Stan Grant is a Wiradjuri and Kamilaroi man. A journalist since 1987, he has worked for the ABC, SBS, the Seven Network and Sky News Australia. From 2001 to 2012 he worked for CNN as an anchor and senior correspondent in Asia and the Middle East. As a journalist, he has received a string of prestigious international and Australian awards. In 2015, he published his bestselling book *Talking to My Country*, which won the Walkley Book Award, and he also won a Walkley Award for his coverage of Indigenous affairs. In 2016 he was appointed to the Referendum Council on Indigenous recognition. Stan is now Chair of Indigenous/ Australian Belonging at Charles Sturt University and International Affairs Analyst at the ABC.

Also by Stan Grant
and published by HarperCollins

The Tears of Strangers
Talking to My Country
Australia Day
With the Falling of the Dusk

The Queen is Dead

STAN GRANT

FOURTH ESTATE

Fourth Estate

An imprint of HarperCollins*Publishers*
Australia • Brazil • Canada • France • Germany • Holland • India
Italy • Japan • Mexico • New Zealand • Poland • Spain • Sweden
Switzerland • United Kingdom • United States of America

HarperCollins acknowledges the Traditional Custodians
of the land upon which we live and work, and pays respect
to Elders past and present.

First published in Australia in 2023
by HarperCollins*Publishers* Australia Pty Limited
Gadigal Country
Level 13, 201 Elizabeth Street, Sydney NSW 2000
ABN 36 009 913 517
harpercollins.com.au

A catalogue record for this book is available from the National Library of Australia

ISBN 978 1 4607 6402 2 (paperback)
ISBN 978 1 4607 1620 5 (ebook)

Cover design by Darren Holt, HarperCollins Design Studio
Author photograph by Kathy Luu
Typeset in Minion Pro by Kirby Jones
Printed and bound in Australia by McPherson's Printing Group

To Baiame, my creator

To Jesus Christ, my saviour

To Yindyamarra, the Spirit

'Vindicate me, O God. And plead my cause against

an ungodly nation.'

– Psalm 43:1

CONTENTS

MY MOTHER'S SON

When the Queen first visited Australia in 1954, my mother almost did not get to see her.

Like millions of other school kids, Mum was expected to join the throng flocking to glimpse the young royal.

The problem was, my mother didn't have any socks.

She was a dirt-poor Aboriginal kid living in a tin humpy on the outskirts of Coonabarabran, in north-west NSW. Socks were a luxury. Clothes and shoes were shared among a dozen siblings.

The school said no socks, no go for the trip to Dubbo to see the Queen. Mum's older brother had made the royal trek a day earlier and met Mum at the back fence between the primary and high schools and threw his socks over.

It is a memory that has stayed with Mum. She has told me the story many times – wearing her brother's cast-off socks to see the Queen.

It is one of the rich memories of a long life. And she has other memories, other stories that she has told me.

Stories of her father being tied to a tree like a dog by police and left all day without food or water to swelter in the sun.

Seeing Aboriginal men arrested for drinking alcohol and roped together and marched down the main street of her hometown.

Stories of two younger brothers who died as children.

Stories of her siblings taken to welfare homes. Stories of aching hunger. Of once following a White girl eating a cake around the schoolyard and pouncing on a crumb that the girl dropped. My mother still says it was the best cake she ever tasted.

The girl with no socks got to see the Queen, while her family and other Black families lived in poverty that the Crown inflicted on them. Living homeless in a land that had been stolen from them in the name of the Crown.

I called my mother this week and she told me the story of her childhood brush with royalty over again. I have thought about Mum and Dad and all of my family, of my people – First Nations people – who die young and live impoverished and imprisoned lives in this country.

We aren't supposed to talk about these things this week. We aren't supposed to talk about colonisation, empire, violence about Aboriginal sovereignty, not even about the republic.

Everyone from the prime minister down has told us it is not appropriate.

I'm sure I am not alone amongst Indigenous people wrestling with swirling emotions. Among them has been anger. The choking asphyxiating anger at the suffering and injustice my people endure.

This anger is not good for me. It is not good for my mental health. It is not good for my physical health. I have been short of breath and dizzy.

But that is nothing compared to what too many other Indigenous people go through day after day. Those languishing in cells. Those who take their own lives. Those who are caught in endless cycles of despair.

Writing this is not good for me. I feel my pulse racing now. I feel the tension building in my head. The veins constricting.

I know what will come. I know the abuse that will come from those who don't like Aboriginal people who speak up.

I know that online trolls will target my family with the most foul language, even threats of physical violence.

Why do we do it? I ask myself that, too. Why do we have to explain ourselves, why do we have to relive pain?

Why? Because a voice is all we have. Because too often that voice is silenced. Like this week.

I have wondered where that voice is. If it has spoken it has more often been in muted tones, lest anyone be offended.

I have wondered where the voices of Indigenous political leadership have been. Where have they been as Indigenous rugby league player Caitlin Moran received a suspension to the equivalent of a quarter of her salary for an Instagram post deemed offensive to the Queen?

Australians will likely vote in a referendum for a constitutionally enshrined Indigenous Voice to Parliament, but what good would that voice be if at times like these it is reduced to a whisper?

This past week, I have been reminded what it is to come from the other side of history. History itself that is written as a hymn to Whiteness.

History written by the victors and often written in blood. It is fashioned as a tale of progress, as a civilising mission.

As historian Caroline Elkins writes in *Legacies of Violence*, her history of the British Empire, for hundreds of millions of people 'the empire's velvet glove contained an all too familiar iron fist'.

From India to Africa to Ireland, the Pacific, the Caribbean

and of course here, Australia, people from the other side of history have felt that fist.

It is not a zero-sum game. There are things in the British tradition that have enriched my life. But history is not weighted on the scales, it is felt in our bones. It is worn on our skin. It is scarred in memory.

How do we live with the weight of this history? How do we not fall prey to soul-destroying vengeance and resentment, yet never relent in our righteous demand for justice?

At times like these I struggle with that dilemma. Because Australia has never reached a just settlement with First Nations people.

But again, we don't talk about that this week.

I have felt a sadness at feeling adrift, estranged from friends and colleagues. Sadness at knowing that at times like these there is a chasm between us.

I have watched as others have worn black and reported on this historic event, participated in this ritual mourning. And knowing I cannot.

They come to this with no conflict. I cannot.

My colleagues can extol the Queen's undoubted and admirable devotion to duty. They can lament the passing of 'everyone's grandmother'.

My thoughts have been on my grandmother.

My people have a word, Yindyamarra – its meaning escapes English translation. It is a philosophy – a way of living – grounded in a deep respect.

I have sought to show Yindyamarra to those for whom this moment is profound. This is their 'sorry business' and I respect that.

But it will pass. For Indigenous people, our sorry business is without end.

At times like these I wonder what it would be to not know apocalypse. To not know what it is to come from a people who face an existential threat. Who have clung on to their very place on this earth.

I wonder what it would be like for me to be like my colleagues for whom this is one of the defining stories of their lifetimes.

Sometimes, I wonder what it must be like to be White.

But then I would not be my mother's son.

Published by ABC News, Sunday, 18 September 2022

2

THE LAST WHITE QUEEN

The White Queen is dead.

Like Cleopatra or Helen of Troy, she is now a thing of history. She is a relic.

It is time to bury her. Not just her body, but the very idea of her. Most importantly the very idea of her.

This is not about the Queen. Not the Queen we knew. Her face as familiar as the faces of our own mothers. It is not about the flesh-and-blood human being. The wife. The mother. The grandmother. It is not about the beautiful princess she once was, nor the dignified, gracious equally beautiful elderly woman she became. It is not about the bright yellow dresses or the decorative hats on race day. It is not about the kindly twinkle in her eye and the reassuring voice every Christmas, in her message from the palace. Like so many others, I will miss that Queen. I will miss her as much as I'd miss a part of myself. The years turn and work their changes on us. The Queen was a constant. Now that constant is gone.

I met that Queen once. Very briefly. She extended her hand, I shook it. Her smile was fixed yet seemingly genuine, and she offered a few words before I moved on. I was as charmed by that Queen as any other who had the pleasure of being introduced to her. That was the Queen fulfilling her duty. The Queen of service and dedication. It mattered little to her, I'm sure, who I was, but more that I was one of hers. A subject. She was my head of state. I lived under her Crown. The laws that governed my life come with her seal of approval. That Queen stared down at us from pubs and clubs and schools and parliaments all across the country. That was the Queen of strength and stay. She was the Queen we were once afforded the opportunity of throwing over and yet did not, could not.

I have known that Queen my entire life. No Australian under the age of seventy has known another. That may have been her appeal – that she was known well enough to not be known. Just the Queen. Just enough for most. I can understand the attraction. I can understand how she was a comfort. The world spins with such force and yet she remained. She came to the throne at the height of empire and watched it decay. She saw tyranny and war. During the Blitz she stood with her people. I know so many loved that Queen. Perhaps, were I them, I might love her too. Perhaps I would like to have had the chance.

I could admire that Queen. That Queen I met briefly so many years ago – and yet it is true that I can remember that moment in every detail. I admire that she remained. That, in the face of scrutiny and loss and disappointment and family indignity, she was steadfast. I like stoicism. I like quiet endurance. I admire that, in her life of service, she even kept a little piece of the world for herself. Wellingtons and wet walks and corgis and horses. I admire that.

This is not about the Queen. But it is about the White Queen. I cannot shake this moment. In her death I feel the world turn. The White Queen is a metaphor. She stands in right now for hundreds of years of an idea of Whiteness. That myth, that trick of the mind, that invention of race. Not real. But oh, how terrifyingly real to most of us on Earth.

I will not mention by name the Queen. The Queen I met. That's our way. We respect the dead and their names. Names changed or never again mentioned. But she will be the White Queen, and that's more important than her name anyway. To me it is the most important thing.

I cannot love the White Queen – the idea. I cannot mourn the White Queen.

The White Queen is dead. May she be the last White Queen.

❈

What do I mean, the last White Queen?

There will never again be a Queen who reigns in a world where Whiteness is so assured. The empire into which she was born and over which she reigned is a thing of nostalgia. Like a cool autumn evening when the sun dips early and the branches of stark trees stripped of their leaves hang still in the breathless air, Britain itself is a thing of faded beauty. I lived there. I know the streets of London. I know her hidden corners. I know her accent. I know the way she laughs. I know her ghosts. I think that anywhere we live becomes a part of us. I have drunk and eaten from her. Her ground has been a pillow. She has filled me up and rested me. For a thousand nights I slept under Britain's stars and felt that I was home. I want that Britain – my Britain – to lay its burden down.

The White Queen is dead. Let the spell be broken.

This spell has been cast for a thousand years. It is an evil magic, a trick of nature that fixes a hierarchy of humanity with people who imagine they are White at the top and those of us deemed not White measured below. Henry VIII, Queen Victoria, William Shakespeare, Thomas Hobbes, Jane Austen, William Blake, Napoleon Bonaparte, Joan of Arc, Ludwig van Beethoven, Wolfgang Amadeus Mozart, Vincent Van Gogh, Marie Curie, Thomas Jefferson, James Cook, Albert Einstein, Sigmund Freud, Friedrich Nietzsche, the Beatles, Alfred Hitchcock, Karl Marx, Adolf Hitler, Hannah Arendt, Madonna, Margaret Thatcher. We have created a world in the image of Whiteness. White monarchs. White scientists. White artists. White poets. White musicians. White thinkers. White terror and White fear. Yes, and White love and White mercy. But still hite. All of it White.

How many names have been erased? How many names we should know but do not. Terence and Tagore, Tenzing and Truganini. Look close enough and they are there. They are not hidden. But more likely they speak against the world and not to it. Across the centuries they wrote words of eternal peace and love, and they led White man to the top of the Earth, and they spoke of resilience and survival. To most, these names are strange. It is those other names, and the countless, countless names of people considered White, that fall so easily from our lips.

I have tried this test on people. In one minute name ten famous people. How easily the names come, how White each person is. In another minute, I ask, name ten who are not White. These people have shaped our world too; their thoughts and faiths and art have fired our imaginations. But they don't come so easily to mind. Muhammad Ali, some say, Nelson Mandela, Martin Luther King, Gandhi. Some might reach further: Beyoncé, Toni Morrison, Oprah Winfrey. Tick … tick … tick … think … Miles Davis, Barack Obama … Chairman Mao. The minute has long passed.

Under the spell of Whiteness, it is White people we see first. The Whitest stars that shine brightest. Interestingly, when I ask someone to name those people who are not White, no one says Jesus. In a world where Whiteness is prized, Jesus – a dark-haired, dark-skinned Jewish man from the Middle East – has become bathed in beatific White splendour.

How many White people are there on Earth? I have asked this question too, and no one gets it right. By some estimates, there are about 700 million people in the world whom we would call Caucasian. You could fit twice that number into China or India. That is fewer than one in ten people. The United Nations says that by 2025, some 98 per cent of the world's population growth will be in non-White countries, particularly Africa and Asia. Gravity is tilting. In 1900 Europe had a quarter of the world's population, but by the middle of the present century that will have fallen to just

7 per cent. By 2050, it is thought one in four people on Earth will be African.

But who is White? Or, better said, who gets to be White? How can you define something that isn't real to begin with? All this talk of colour and race is invented. Some people deemed White today were not considered White yesterday. The Irish, Greeks, some Hispanic people. We are not talking about a colour but an idea. It is an idea of power. For centuries power has been given a face, and that face is coloured White.

How many White people are there? When I ask that question, the number never fails to astonish. Because Whiteness is all around us. It is a swarm. All-seeing, all-knowing Whiteness. And where we are engulfed by Whiteness, all else dims. I have tried this on people who are not considered White. I have asked them that same question: how many White people are there on Earth? I see their eyes widen, their mouths fall open, when they hear the answer. It is a moment of clarity. The scales fall from their eyes; they wonder, what have we been so afraid of?

Fewer than 10 per cent of the people in the world are White: Caucasian.

Why are we so surprised? This is the trick. Whiteness is an illusion. We fail to see what is right in front of us. There are far more of us who are not White than those who are. But we are hypnotised by Whiteness. We see it even when it is not there. Because it is everywhere. It frames everything. We live in a maze of mirrors and each one distorts our reality. Once trapped in Whiteness, we cannot easily find our way out. And in each warped mirror, Whiteness stares back at us.

Such a tiny number of White people have conquered the world. And I do mean conquered. With force and their law, they have subdued the planet. Whiteness has bent the world to its will. Are these people who think themselves White so supernaturally gifted? Are they chosen by the gods? Do they possess some wisdom unknown to the rest of us? No. The conquest of Whiteness is no divine providence. It is no accident. It was drawn on maps. It was sailed on ships. It was written in books. It was weighed in gold. It was marched in columns. It was sounded off in cannon fire. It was hoist by flags. It was named empire.

❖

Of all the things known about the Queen, of all the things written about the Queen, this is the most important: that she was White. It is the most important thing to me. She was the epitome of Whiteness. Without Whiteness, she would not have been Queen. And no one who is not White has ever sat on that throne.

Let me repeat it, and say it slowly: the White Queen is dead.

It sounds like the beginning of a fairytale. And that's what it is. Fairytales and magic. As with all fairytales, we believe it because we want to believe. And like all fairytales, its power is enchantment. We want to hold on to the dream of a beautiful young princess who meets her handsome prince, and together they live their days in grand castles with servants and have their own family of White princes and princesses.

In this fairytale, only the fairest in the land rule over the kingdom.

I can feel some readers bristling already. I have called the Queen White. It sounds impolite. It sounds like an insult. It is not meant to be. There is the Queen and there is the White Queen. There are many kings and queens in our world, some of them White, but there is only one White Queen. She is monarch above all monarchs. Think about this: we don't even have to mention her by name, as she is simply *the Queen*. As if there is no other. She is the epitome of what it is to be White, ruling from an invented White land.

For the first time but not the last, I will say it: Whiteness is not about White people (even though so many White people may convince us otherwise). There are White people who have stared into the face of Whiteness and said no! White people who have paid with their own blood to end the grim fairytale of Whiteness. Many of the people who speak to me, who inspire me, are White. Who have been told they are White. Who believe they are White. There are people who believe they are White, and there are the rest of us, who are told we are not. I can love people who believe they are White even as I cannot love Whiteness itself. They are trapped too. They are in their own maze of mirrors, where their reflection stares back at them as creation. The world is their own creation. Everything in their image. But they are doomed. The Greeks told us that. Narcissus spurned all but his own reflection, the love of himself that could not be returned, and he melted away. The rest of us remain an echo in the forest.

White people cannot be free while ever Whiteness rules.

The White Queen is dead. The last White Queen.

3

THE TURNING

T he White Queen is dead.

Her death marks a turning point. Around the world there is a reckoning with Whiteness. The North Star of Whiteness is dimming. Everywhere the legacy of empire, the legacy of Whiteness, is contested. It is volatile. It is unpredictable. It swings wildly from left to right, from hope to despair. There is no road map. The answers of the twentieth century can't solve the riddles of the twenty-first. Democracy is in retreat. It has lost its moral core. Democracy has been captured by big money and big power. It cannot speak to the voices that demand to be heard. Demagogues exploit anxiety and fear, fan racism and xenophobia to claim power. These false prophets promise to return nations to some fantasy of former glory.

Authoritarianism is on the march. Barbed wire is going back up on the borders of Europe. Brown-skinned refugees fleeing wars of empire are being turned away or locked up in detention centres. White supremacist far-right political groups are finding fertile ground. Hitler-admiring neo-fascists are in the German parliament. The White underclass are left behind, no longer sure of the countries they live in and looking for someone to blame. Black Lives Matter protests have shaken the world. Statues of blood-stained imperialists – many the White Queen's ancestors – are coming down. Athletes are taking a knee. Misogyny and homophobia are being called out, as voices too long silenced demand to be heard. As Yeats wrote, 'the blood-dimmed tide is loosed'.

Whiteness as an organising principle is exhausted. It is weighed down by history. History, the very thing it created, is turning to strike with a vengeance. The pillars of Whiteness – liberalism and democracy – buckle under the strain. They weren't designed for this. Born out of the eighteenth-century Enlightenment, they were conceived as a way of bringing order to chaos. They prized forgetting as a pathway to freedom. Liberalism severed the bonds between faith and family and tradition. Thinkers such as Immanuel Kant captured the Enlightenment in his phrase 'dare to know'. To imagine our own futures. To look beyond the horizons to a view from nowhere. The world had been torn apart by wars of religion. Kant believed we could create a world of perpetual peace. Humans have spent three centuries chasing that elusive dream.

Whiteness has made war on itself. Each time promising a new reign of peace, only to plunge in to war again. Ever more devastating war. Liberalism, fascism, socialism, communism: each has competed with its own utopian vision. Each has descended into terror and tyranny. Each has been put in service of power. Each was born out of the imagination of a White man. White men have written our future: Thomas Hobbes, John Locke, David Hume, Jean-Jacques Rousseau, John Stuart Mill, Georg Wilhelm Friedrich Hegel, Karl Marx, each of them offering a vision of what it is to be human. They invented modernity as a place of endless possibility.

They saw the hand of God in humanity's progress. God guided the pen but it was humans who could now write their own destiny. These moderns were a rip in the order of things. God was the ghost in the machine of human reason. Now reason was theirs. It was the slave of their passions. If man was made of crooked timber, then reason and time, history, would make him straight. In time, men would be gods themselves. These so-called enlightened beings were deciding who was human. They spoke of men, not women – and they spoke of White, not Black.

Of all the dreams of these men, it is liberalism that has proved the most resilient and seductive. As the twentieth century neared its end, liberal democracy crowned itself triumphant. The Cold War was ended, the Soviet Union had crumbled, and communism appeared lifeless. New nations had emerged from behind the Iron Curtain and were embracing freedom. This was hailed as the very end of history itself. For that brief moment, there were no more struggles to be had. We were all, so it was said, on a journey to the same destination. Liberalism sought to defy gravity. Its weightlessness allowed it to change shape, to float where other ideologies sank. In the rare air of liberalism, we could breathe each other in without also inhaling the toxic fumes of the past, of identity or enmity.

That's the dream, anyway.

The White Queen is dead and I am listening to a debate between two men on the merits of liberalism and conservatism. They are persuasive. They are decent. They listen and respond to each other with respect. At times I find myself agreeing with each of them. The liberal talks about liberty, about the rights of individuals. We should be free to determine our own destiny. He says people should not be judged on colour. He doesn't want to peer into our bedrooms. He is gay, and he should be free to be who he is – but he should not be defined by his sexuality or his gender. I find myself nodding along. The conservative talks about tradition. He says our society is a compact across the generations. Each one upholding and preserving what binds us. Culture is important. Faith. Family. Yes. To me those things are precious.

There is so much I can agree with, but then I stop short. I know they are not talking about me. They are talking about the world Whiteness made. Both these men are White. The world was designed for them. It was written by White men just like them. They talk about values – but whose values? The culture they defend – whose culture? Never once do they imagine what life might look like for someone like me.

I actually find myself wishing I could be like them. That the world could be a choice between freedom and tradition. If only these things were debating points. If only this was not a question of life and death. If only. I wouldn't have to feel like an outsider. I could be as assured as they are. But it all stops at the water's edge of history. Of race. Of course they can imagine a world without racism – because they invented it. Of course they can triumph over history – for they have written it. Yes, tradition matters – because tradition has been the source of their power. To me it all sounds so cold. It is so bloodless.

We could all don a veil of ignorance and construct a theoretical Valhalla. This was the dream of another White thinker, John Rawls. Here we would be unaware of gender, sexuality, faith or race. Here rights would not be weighted based on who you were but distributed neutrally. If there was to be bias, let its benefits flow to the neediest. It sounds almost too perfect, and it is. It is the imagined end point of the *mission civilisatrice* – the civilising mission. It is also, conveniently, White. After hundreds of years of exporting – mostly violently – the liberal dreams of White men, Whiteness slips the knot. It makes a virtue of its power.

But liberalism's strength was always its weakness. Who can shake off the dust from our ancestors' journeys? In our congested, contested world, we are running into ourselves and straining to fit. Liberalism – weightless and neutral – has no ballast. There is just the mantra of freedom, which for the greatest number in the world has always carried the echo of gunfire.

✳

The White Queen is dead.

War is raging in Ukraine. Vladimir Putin is seeking to redraw the map of Europe. He has his own dreams of empire. He wants to avenge history. To turn back the clock. To Putin, Ukraine will never be European – it is Russian. Putin's war is not just on Ukraine; it is a war on an idea. Putin has prophets of hatred whispering in his ear. They tell him of Russia's golden age. They speak about catastrophe. Never forget the humiliation of the twentieth century, they tell him. To them, Whiteness has become decadent. The West – that other trick of the mind, a place invented, not real – is crumbling. It doesn't work anymore. Truth is buried under a torrent of noise. Was there ever truth at all? God is dead. The family has lost its moral core. The poor get poorer and the rich get richer. These Russian philosophers imagine a revitalised *Russkiy mir* – a Russian world. They are not of the West: they are not White as the West is White, but Eurasian.

Putin listens. He has a bitter taste of history.

This is the sort of war the West does not know how to fight. Yes, it can bring guns and money, but this isn't just about firepower. It is not just about territory, or borders, or resources, or power. It is existential: it is about identity. Not identity as some mean it – something to choose, to change, to put on and cast off like a suit of clothes. Identities can nourish us. They can give us community. Identities can give us voice. That notion of identity is a conceit of the West – identity as freedom. But identity can also – and far more often than not, in fact – be a pathway to tyranny.

To Vladimir Putin, identity is primal. It is written on the soul. He has made it clear that Ukraine is part of the soul of

Russia. And he is prepared to crush the souls of Ukrainians to achieve his ends. Why? Because to Putin, there is no Ukraine without Russia. They are one. It is blood and it is soil. It is spiritual. *Russkiy mir* is holy: and central is the Russian Orthodox faith. To Russian nationalists like Putin, Ukraine's capital, Kyiv, is the mother of all Russian cities.

Putin famously called the collapse of the Soviet Union 'the greatest geopolitical catastrophe of the twentieth century'. It is oft repeated, but not as often understood. Putin doesn't want communism back: he wants Russia back. The catastrophe wasn't the collapse of Marxist Leninism, it was the suffering of the people. Russian-speaking Slavic people were cut adrift – as Putin sees it – from Mother Russia.

It is a vengeful vision, for sure, but it comes from somewhere very real. Yes, Russia was humiliated. The West's triumph morphed into hubris. The West claimed the hand of God in the end of the Cold War: this was a victory over evil itself. The Evil Empire. But the West in these moments ignores the bones piled at its own feet. It ignores the wreckage left by the wayside as it marches forward. The history of the world is the last judgement, and that judgement is the province of the victor. But the souls of the vanquished don't rest. Listen to the words of Schiller:

What future is't that graves to us reveal?

What the eternity of thy discourse?

Honoured because dark veils its forms conceal,

The giant-shadows of the awe we feel,

Viewed in the hollow mirror of remorse!

Here is the price of freedom. The dark veils it conceals. Hidden by its hollow remorse. Freedom, we are told, is the price worth paying. Who can argue with freedom?

The West may yet win. For the sake of the people of Ukraine, we can only hope it does. But what would that victory mean? Will Western powers congratulate themselves? Will they see as this another divine triumph of Western will? There is danger there. Because the seeds of resentment will grow more conflict. Wars of identity don't end. They come again. And again and again.

The West's promise of freedom – glorious as it is – leaves us unhinged. Unsettled and disoriented. Angry. Because the freedom of Whiteness is a lie to so many. And in that space between the promise of freedom and the lie of freedom are the graveyards of history.

Here is something I have come to know: history and identity are twin heads of a serpent.

Osama bin Laden had the same bitter taste of the past. People whispered in his ear too. They had their own catastrophic visions. They told him about empire. About White Empires that carved up Arab and Muslim lands. About the Ottoman Empire and its collapse and disgrace. Muslims looked to the West, too, captured by ideas of democracy. Yet so many found only a rotting core. Decadence. Hypocrisy. Power. I have had these conversations in Muslim lands, battlegrounds of seemingly unending wars. I have sat down with imams and fighters. I have sat in madrassas – Islamic schools – watching boys rocking back and forth for hours on end as their teacher reads the Koran and beats time with a stick. Under the floorboards of the same madrassas police have found suicide bombers' vests, filled with explosives.

Don't think this is all Muslims. Far from it. Not even a majority. Muslims – innocent people, women and old people and children – have been the biggest casualties in the so-called war on terror. Never have I experienced so warm a welcome and such hospitality as I have in the homes and lands of Muslim friends. But there is a shadow on that world. And I walked in those shadows where Bin Laden walked too, buying more converts, arming them, leading them into foreign wars. For decades he wove a web of terror. He waited. He plotted. On 11 September 2001 he struck at the heart of the great empire, the citadel of democracy and the capital of capitalism. The world has been reeling ever since. War. Economic collapse. Political upheaval. Pandemic. Osama bin Laden did not orchestrate this. He did not even set the wheels in motion. That would be to give him too grand a place in history. But he was at its roiling heart.

Xi Jinping has a grand seat at history's banquet. Like Putin and Bin Laden, Xi feasts on the past. Like them, he has the bread of apocalypse in his mouth. Xi too tells his people of humiliation. A century of humiliation. Never forget what these foreign powers have done, he says. He is fighting old wars. Xi wants to avenge a war with Britain that happened a century before he was born. The Opium Wars triggered the collapse of the Qing Empire. It was China's dark night of the soul. Ahead lay a hundred years of revolution, rebellion, bloodshed almost without equal.

In 1997 I stood in the driving rain on the border of Hong Kong and the China mainland. A convoy farther than my eye could see brought the troops of the People's Liberation Army to reclaim what China had lost. One by one the trucks and armoured personnel carriers passed me, soldiers standing erect as the rain pelted down. Some saluted. This was a triumph for China and not a shot had been fired. The humiliation was being avenged. Moments like these recast our world. There in the rain I could feel history turn. The handover of Hong Kong from Britain to China marked an end of empire and a renewal of empire. That night kick-started the twenty-first century. China has returned as a global power and Britain has faded. It could not be lost on anyone who watched the British flag lowered how easily empires fall. Slowly and then so fast.

For a quarter of a century I have written about, read about, and reported on and in China. No place has captivated me more. And I can feel in the land itself all the restlessness of its history. I hear it when people say they will eat bitterness. I have found there the whisper of my own home. It is a place of ghosts, and I know about ghosts.

Xi Jinping hears the whisper of ghosts too. He imagines himself a great man of history. He has his mind on destiny. He believes he will be the last great leader of China, finishing what those who have come before him began. It is within his grasp. And the world has awoken to this now.

This scares the West. It scares Whiteness. China does not just represent a power shift – this is the first time in three hundred years that a White nation is not the Earth's most powerful. White Western nations that have so tightly controlled power now blame China for seeking to do the same. They criticise China for wiping out minorities. Xi Jinping is accused of genocide. I have been to these places where China's heavy hand crushes the spirit of its own people. I have seen the brave souls standing up to power. And paying a dreadful cost. Yet I cannot but see in China what White nations have done the world over. Genocide is genocide. Under their flags, nations committed to Whiteness have erased entire populations, mine included. They have not been held to account. No, genocide is a word they reserve for others.

The West is comfortable with the suffering of people if it furthers the interests of its own power. Let anyone who has walked the same roads as me try to deny that. The nations that so accuse China today of human rights abuses have propped up despots and funded tyranny. At home, the West's myths of equality and democracy and rights land, for so many, with a dull thud. I can hear people now, the great defenders of the West, say: but where would you rather be? I have been asked this so many times. I know what comes next too: I should be grateful. I heard someone on television – a journalist, a writer – say that I should be thankful that Captain Cook 'discovered' Australia, otherwise I would not be able to write. Yes, the ability to read and to spell is apparently fair trade for the slaughter of my people and the theft of our land.

Where would I rather be? As if I have a choice. That was taken from my ancestors with invasion. But here I am and yes, here somewhere amid this ruin, this hypocrisy, there is still something to cherish. Because freedom – freedom still just out of reach – is not White. Because liberty is not White. Because people the world over have held tight to those ideals. Because people who were transported in slave ships; who were slapped in chains; who had their lands stolen; those people shine a light for me. Because ideas of fraternity and equality belong to us all. Because the dreams of peace that emerged out of war and revolution belong to us all. Because this is my birthright too. And because my people have paid such a price for it. Because the people who lay claim to these ideas as their own, as their gift to humanity, have so often betrayed those ideas. These things do not belong only to the West. These things are human. The Enlightenment is the West's legacy but it is not the preserve of Whiteness. The great thinkers of the West rolled back the horizon but not always for the good. Yes, I would rather be here because Whiteness can be held to account. Its own portentous liberty can be shone like a bright light into the face of Whiteness itself.

My grandfather used to keep by his bed the Bible and the works of Shakespeare. He fought for this country in the Second World War. He raised his children to know there is a place for them in this world, and that others cannot define that. He raised them proud of being Wiradjuri. But being Wiradjuri did not mean to not explore other cultures and ideas. He was not a man who scorned the West even as he lived under the yoke of colonisation. He knew we were all fallen and frail. We were possessed, he once wrote, of all the vices and virtues of humanity. We are human, not better or worse: human.

My memories of him are faint. He died when I was young. But he is in me. And he is with me. I have tried to live by his example. Like him, I know the West is a place of wonder. The West has tilted at the universal. The revolutions of the West ripped open the world and created new ideas about what it is to be a human. Its art, its literature, its architecture – these have been things of endless inspiration to me. I have rarely been as moved as when I stood in the Sistine Chapel, humbled by Michelangelo's devotion. The image of Adam and God, hands reaching for each other yet their fingers never touching, is the struggle within all of us, not just to find the transcendent but to reach each other.

But we make a mistake when we imagine that the West is a place. Or that it is a people. Or that it is White. Especially if we think it is White. It is a place created. It is only the West because it faces peoples elsewhere. I am in the West, but can I say I am of it? No. And I don't need to. Like my grandfather, I can take from it but never accept that it is the province of Whiteness. Nor do I have to be White.

Yes, I will take those words of empire – that 'gift' of Whiteness – and use them to speak back. Because these people who demand I be grateful don't get to tell me the truth.

That's why they fear China. Because China knows the truth of empire. Strip away all the politics, all of the 'whataboutism', and we are left with brutality. The brutality of empires throughout time. Brutality that Xi Jinping now emulates. The West looks at China and is disturbed by what it sees looking back. Because China is a mirror. These nations, bathed in their own Whiteness, recognise in China something of themselves. China is a creation of the West even as it emerged out of defeat by the British Empire. Modern China is built out of empire. The rise of empire and the fall of empire. China had for thousands of years thought itself to be the centre of the universe. Kings and emperors made tribute. And then it all ended.

The fall of the Qing Empire in the nineteenth century hastened a racial reckoning for the Chinese. And it also brought China face to face with White power. The Qing Empire was humbled by Britain, a tiny island that now occupied Chinese territory. For Chinese thinkers, this was the moment to chart a new course. The nineteenth-century writer Yan Fu was influenced by European liberal thinkers such as John Stuart Mill and the father of economics, Adam Smith, and saw China's future as being to emulate Western liberalism.

Perhaps the most influential thinker of all, Liang Qichao, also looked to the Western idea of history as a march of progress – and progress meant modernisation. Liang is known as the godfather of Chinese nationalism. His acolytes included the Chinese communist revolutionary leader Mao Zedong.

Liang coined the phrase 'the sick man of Asia' to capture China's fallen state. He said the Chinese had awoken from a thousand-year-long dream. As Liang embraced Western ideas, he also advocated the unity of the 'yellow race'. He used the term *minzu* to describe the people of the nation. The First World War was another reckoning. At the Paris peace talks after the First World War, China felt abandoned. German-occupied Chinese territory was handed back not to China but to Japan. The seeds of resentment were sown.

The historian Jerome Ch'en wrote that 'from 1842 to 1942, China had been treated by the West with distrust, ridicule, and disdain'. Liang Qichao, who had looked to the West, now turned away. He was an official observer in Paris but returned believing that to follow the West would lead China to catastrophe.

At the same time, the world was warning of the 'yellow peril'. Australia had its own Whites-only policy, adopted to exclude non-White races from the country. Racial politics was also shaping China's great foe, Japan. The Japanese derided the

Chinese as 'yellow'. Japan saw itself as being on a par with Western powers. Its imperialism emulated the imperialism of the White colonisers.

For hundreds of years, power and Whiteness have been synonymous. From the British Empire to the American Century, White nations have exported violence, committed genocide, stolen land and made it all legal. China, like so many other non-White nations, has felt the sting of White imperialism. Chinese leaders have seen their struggle in racial terms. Mao Zedong styled himself as a revolutionary leader of the non-White world. His military strategies have been adopted by the Viet Cong, the Taliban, al-Qaeda and Islamic State.

Deng Xiaoping travelled to Europe as a young man and saw the racial discrimination against Chinese people there. His economic revolution was built on beating the West at its own game. Xi Jinping lectures the West on its own hypocrisy. He is still fighting the Opium Wars against Britain, the fall of the Qing – the great humiliation. His dream is to return China to the apex of global power. China today is seen as a threat to the West. A threat to the so-called 'global rules-based order', which is rooted in a race-based order.

It is not possible to understand China without understanding race and racism. Specifically, without understanding Whiteness. Yet far too often the conversation around the rise of this new superpower is about geopolitics. It is about authoritarianism versus democracy. About human rights. About whether we will go to war. But race sits at the heart of it all. China looks at the alliance of Western nations, such as the AUKUS agreement – Australia, the UK and the US – and sees a race-based military bloc of White countries. China's ambassador to Australia, Xiao Qian, said that's how it appears to people in other countries. What he means is non-White countries. The Chinese Communist Party has a deep racial consciousness.

I share that consciousness. I know what they know. When I hear White people talk about China, there is always something missing. They simply cannot grasp what it is to not be White. But as I share the view from the other side of history I have to resist the lure of resentment. I have to. I cannot allow that to define me. There is no virtue in the resentment held by the likes of Xi and Putin and Bin Laden. History for them is an open wound. They pick at it time and again. This septic history is who they are; they would not know themselves without it.

Yet I cannot deny its pull. I am wounded too. And I know those wounds will not, cannot heal. And part of me – the wounded part – does not want to heal. I want those who have driven the blade to see what they have done. But I have seen, too, where resentment leads. I have followed the murder of innocence. I have seen what happens when evil answers evil.

❖

The White Queen is dead.

If Britain invented Whiteness, then the United States of America was the first White country. Conceived and birthed in Whiteness. Britain's gift to the world. Its child, which would violently rebel and then extend the empire. A nation conceived as White. Slaughter of non-White people. Enslavement of non-White people. And all of it a dream. A dream of Whiteness.

America's dreams are tortured. The bloodletting of the Civil War – brother on brother, neighbour on neighbour – was the price for living out its creed. Making good on equality. This war to free the slaves. White people fighting White people, sacrificing for others. So goes the White heroes myth. In truth, it was as self-serving as noble. A war to protect the Union, not shatter it. States' rights. Economic rights. White rights. White heroes.

Lincoln freed the slaves? No, he didn't – slaves freed the slaves. Yes, the president signed the Emancipation Proclamation, but it was Black people who defied the whip. Black people who sang their freedom. Black people who never believed what the White slave masters said about them. Should we even call them slaves? That's not how they saw themselves. The slaves were those who were chained to their Whiteness. Chained to their supposed superiority. The so-called slaves shamed America. If Abraham Lincoln knew anything, he knew that abolishing slavery was the price for keeping America. By his second inaugural, with his nation torn asunder and the bloodletting continuing, he saw his work as God's work. Perhaps this was God's reckoning with a nation bathed in the evil of human bondage. This was the price America had to pay. The war would continue for as long as God deemed it. Lincoln then pledged to bind up the nation's wounds.

And then America made a myth of tragic White figures. Statues were erected to defeated White Southern Generals. They are silent sentinels of the lost cause, promising that the South will rise again. And White southerners put on White hoods to terrorise 'freed' Blacks. White slaveholders were compensated, not Black people. They have never been paid. What Blacks got was Jim Crow laws enforcing their segregation and consigning them to another century of state-sanctioned racism.

In America, Whiteness now feels under siege. The numbers are against it. Under 60 per cent of the country is considered White. If you don't include some Hispanics, it falls below 50 per cent. In any case, the tide is turning. But Whiteness dies hard. Its evil has waged war with the nation's better angels. America has been humanity's last great hope. The shining city on the hill. Or so it has said. But there has always been another

America. To many – to the Black, the Brown, and the poor – it is a more real America. In that America, power and wealth are held in the hands of a few. America has not had royalty, but it has had an aristocracy: the robber barons of the Gilded Age, the blue-blood families: Carnegie, Rockefeller and Vanderbilt. The brutal truth is that the American Dream, for most people, is just that. To be born poor is to stay poor. Beyond the downtown skyscrapers is a hinterland of desolate strip malls, windswept main streets, polluted duck ponds, playgrounds devoid of the laughter of children.

The last two decades of terrorism, foreign wars, financial crisis and racial strife have accelerated America's decline. It is tired, angry and divided. I have caught trains across the country and stared out the window at miles and miles of emptiness. Desolation. Houses with the doors hanging off the hinges. Lawns overgrown. Wrecked cars. I ask myself, what holds this together, is the dream this strong? No. The lie holds it together. A beautiful lie it may be but a lie no less. No American president will emerge from these neighbourhoods. Not a White one let alone a Black or Brown one. Barack Obama was an aberration. Father from Kenya, a White middle-class mother, raised by White grandparents, educated at private school and Ivy League university, backed by wealthy Chicago political players. This is not the Black experience.

Some in this American wasteland may get lucky. Sport, entertainment or education may be a ticket out. But that's a lottery. For most, they will die where they lived. They will find their happiness as they can. Faith and family may ease the desperation. But sitting on the train I can feel pounding in the collective consciousness of this America. There are fewer flags hanging in the windows. I wonder, would these people fight for this America? What would they even be fighting for? If they believe in the dream at all it is because reality is just too brutal to bear. The American Century is over. Whatever America's future, it won't be as glorious as its past.

In truth, America's has been a slow unravelling. Since the 1960s – a time of tumult, revolution, assassination, flowers and free love, high-pressure hoses and snarling dogs and marches and sit-ins and non-violence and by any means necessary – America has searched for fresh purpose. For a new social contract. Running through it all was the colour line. There was always the promise – taunting as much as tantalising – of getting rich. Class could be transcended. But race was more fixed. One drop of Black blood was enough to make you Black. And the people who thought they were White have always had their ears tuned to the siren call of racism.

Donald Trump squeezed every putrid gasp out of American racism to take himself to the White House. Eight years of the first Black president, Barack Obama, were followed by a tumultuous term of Trumpism. Trump does not speak of the American Dream but, as he said, of 'American carnage'. Why would people believe in America? Obama's hope did not deliver. Many felt betrayed. The nation's fault lines of class, race, and geography deepened. In America, fate is determined by zip codes. In some states, the factories have closed: the work has gone and is never coming back. There is an opioid epidemic. An orgy of gun violence. Suicide. For the first time in a century, in the richest nation the world has ever known, life expectancy has gone backwards. That's the America Trump speaks to. Trump speaks to the dying heart of America.

Maybe America has always been a mirage. From a distance it is so dazzling. A fast world. Fast food and fast cars. Who couldn't fall for Hollywood and Manhattan? America could make the obscene appear beautiful. *Gone With the Wind* brought glamour and romance to slave plantations. Generations of film-goers cheered for John Wayne slaughtering the Indians. Stephen Sondheim made us all want to live there: 'Everything free in America', everything the immigrant wants: a car, a TV, a fridge. Skyscrapers bloom and Cadillacs zoom. But Sondheim – and the Brown-skinned people of his *West Side Story* – knew the eternal truth: 'Life is all right in America, if you're all-White in America.'

❋

The White Queen is dead.

She came to power to the strains of 'Rule Britannia', but she died with Britain unruly: divided at home and weak abroad. Her country is unsure of itself, soothed by memories of past glory. There is a Britain lost in time, where it did not have to apologise for itself. Where its flag was not smeared by the hatred of White supremacists. There is a Britain that will carry on. That will fight them on the beaches and never surrender. There is a Britain of Carnaby Street and Union Jack suits and the Kinks and the Rolling Stones and the Beatles. Some Britons look to this old, lost Britain, and wallow in imperial nostalgia. Did it ever exist, this 'Cool Britannia', this 'British Bulldog'? No. It is a myth, like all national myths. A myth like Whiteness itself.

Around the world, the crypts of history are creaking open. The dead are rising, spilling out of every sealed vault of empire. Spectres are haunting us. The French philosopher Jacques Derrida coined the term 'hauntology' to describe how the past hovers over our present like a ghost. How right he was. And Whiteness quivers in fear of history. It should. These spirits that are stirring are wounded and restless. They are vengeful. These ghosts are hungry. The rattle of their chains can be heard in every darkened corner of our world.

Ghost stories are always a warning. They are about now, not then. They are about us, who we are, not the faint traces and smoky forms that slide in and out of the walls. What we see – what we glimpse out of the corners of our eyes – is ourselves. Spectres live in our imaginings. They are conjured out of our own conscience. They are a shadow world of our own making. These are the ghosts that haunt the world now. These are the ghosts hissing at the world now.

Whiteness gathers dust and bones. Its museums are stockpiled with the trinkets and treasures of the vanquished. Rubies and marbles and things of stone and wood, sacks of loot, the spoils of war, rings pilfered from corpses – and, in the depths of these macabre mausoleums, the corpses themselves. The severed hands and heads of the victims from the other side of history. History is sealed shut. It is put into cold storage. That's how Whiteness likes it. The past is a curiosity, carefully curated. Each item on display. History, for White people, is a pleasant Sunday afternoon, a wander through hallways and exhibits and then tea and scones. History they can see and sometimes touch, but never feel. History to be admired, but never accounted for.

Whiteness doesn't have history – it has time. This time is marked in events, often bloody events. History is a slaughterhouse. But that tragedy and sacrifice is in service of utopia. There is always, for Whiteness, the glimpse of the end of history. Here everything is subdued, straightened, pacified. But time marches forward. This is not history but historicism. It is what Whiteness does with history. It washes the blood from the walls. History is a straight road for those deemed White. For me it is a roundabout, an endless loop; my ancestors are always there and I am always coming around to meet myself.

If we can bury history, we need never study our own reflection. I can see how tempting that is. History can be a pitiless place. It is a trapdoor. There is nothing to break our fall. No soft place to land. We cannot undo it, or remake it. We are in freefall, reaching for branches of hope or justice or restitution, but each remains just out of our grasp. Better to leave history alone. But we cannot. Not those of us for whom history is not a sepia-toned photograph but shards of broken glass.

4

EXILE

The White Queen is dead.

And so I am here as our world stumbles. I am a pilgrim from the other side of history. And I am reminded now that my life has been a journey through the byways of history.

I recall thirty years ago, standing in my cousin's backyard. It is night and all the stars are out. A big, cinematic Australian sky. No, a Wiradjuri sky. A sky with nothing to block out its beauty. My cousin asks: *Will you miss this?* Mmm. Without saying it, I wonder if I will even see the same stars. I haven't lived upside down before, at the other end of the world, but soon I will leave this place and I don't know if I will come back.

It is no surprise that I left Australia. I suppose I was always leaving. I have moved around so much that moving is freedom. I never wanted for home. Home was always with me. All around me. Home is not something I can fence off. That's what an exile is, someone for whom home is a memory ... a feeling. But the exile can't stay at home. I was in Baghdad once, talking to a man who had fled his home in old Palestine. He had never been able to go back. But he brought out a jar filled with sand and put it in my hand. This is my home, he said. I have never carried a jar with me, but home was always there. I just couldn't be free there.

I have always gravitated to the exiles. Those who have gone in search of themselves in a place beyond certainty. James Baldwin, who left America for Paris to be free. To be, he said, not merely a Negro or a Negro writer. Black, yes. But not anyone's idea of Black. Save me from that mystical Black bullshit, he once said. I know what he meant. When I feel the expectations of others – of what I should be – that's when I feel the walls closing in on me. Baldwin did not want to be Black and special any more than to be White is to be special. That's to buy into the lie of race. The myth. The superstition. I don't want any of it.

Those who call themselves classical liberals would tell me that's what modernity offers us: a place beyond race. But that doesn't convince me either. It did not convince James Baldwin. Because he knew something that I have learned: that liberalism is inseparable from race. Liberalism is a shell game. It appears to make race disappear, but the truth is it's just hidden under a veil of Whiteness. However attractive the idea of liberalism may be – and it is attractive to me – my liberalism stops at the water's edge of Whiteness.

Franz Kafka asked how could he identify with the Jews when he could not identify with himself. I ask myself the same things. What is it to be Aboriginal? What on Earth does that word even mean? It was not our word. If I ask my father, he would say he is Wiradjuri. That means something. It is connected to place and kin and culture. It means something to me too. It means that wherever I may go, I have a home. I have a story. Being Kamilaroi means something to me. It comes from my mother. I am connected to all of the many peoples of this land. I am all of those things and I am me. Complicated. Contradictory.

As I write this at a table in a cafe, I watch some of my people wander across the road. They are raucous and funny and full of life. They throw their heads back in laughter and the kids dodge the oncoming cars. And I smile. That was me. It is me, still. But there's another truth. There is a space between us. My travels, my work, my wealth and my privilege have taken me from my own. Those things have taken me even from my blood, my family. They have taken me from myself.

Should these people – my people – trust me? I am not sure I always trust myself. They would do well to be wary of the so-called Black elite; the Black middle class. I am part of it and I know the seductions of economic success. Not that we are less Aboriginal; not that we are not deserving but I know the compromises I have had to make. We make a mistake if we think that individual success is the measure of progress. We risk becoming part of the problem. For whatever I have achieved, my people remain the most impoverished and imprisoned in Australia.

I can't help thinking I have betrayed my own people. White people have used my so-called success to tell others they could do it too. There have been times I have gone along with that. I have thought that a good education, a better job, a secure home are the answer. But whatever we call success, it has come at a price for me. I have made my own bargain with tyranny. Every day I have to negotiate; I have to navigate a space that is not mine. For all that I may have gained I have also lost a bit of my soul. No material wealth can equal the love and kinship and belonging that I can only find among my own people. I look at my life now and I feel so lonely. Only when I am at home on my country, feeling the touch of my own people, do I feel at peace.

I don't speak for Indigenous people. I would not even presume to speak for my own family. Why do I write? Because I cannot but write. And it is all I have to honour those I love. I am a Wiradjuri-Kamilaroi-Dharrawal person; I come from a family with strong cultural roots. I am what my people have made me. I feel a deep kinship and shared struggle with other First Nations people but I don't know what it is to be them. When I hear some speak, I don't always recognise myself. That's ok. I don't know what it is to be Kenyan or Mongolian or Lithuanian or Egyptian either. But we share a world and I have travelled enough to know that there is no barrier to friendship; no barrier to love. We are human.

I have so many questions, questions that confront me with uncertainty and ambiguity. I need to live free of boxes. Free of what others might think I am. I like what Édouard Glissant said when he spoke of the poetics of relation. He didn't believe we are rooted anywhere. There is no one thing that holds us to the Earth. But our roots are entwined, wrapped around each other. This man, who was descended from slaves, saw even the slave ship as a journey to something new.

That is true. Yet without justice those roots entwined can strangle us. My roots are deep in our soil and they are wrapped around the roots of others who now call this place – Australia – home. Foreign ships have brought new people to this land and

I cannot deny they are a part of me. Even if I sometimes may wish it were not so. I am certain of who I am and where I come from. On Wiradjuri or Kamilaroi land I know I belong. Australia as a nation feels like an imposition. And I am sad about that because I want to fill that space between us.

But for now I am drawn to the exiles, those who go and exiles like Toni Morrison, who stayed where she was and looked for that place of freedom in the cracks.

❖

The White Queen is dead.

I am hearing all of those voices of exile. I hear Frederick Douglass ask: 'What, to the American slave, is your Fourth of July?' A day that 'reveals, more than all other days in the year, the gross injustice and cruelty' to which he was 'the constant victim'. To the slave, America's celebration was a 'sham', its 'boasted liberty' an 'unholy licence', its 'national greatness' mere 'swelling vanity', its 'shout of liberty and equality, hollow mockery'.

I know he is talking about my country too.

I hear William Edward Burghardt Du Bois tell me that the problem of the twentieth century was the problem of the colour line. And, I tell myself, so it is still for the twenty-first century. I hear the Reverend Dr Martin Luther King Jr – not the dreamer but the hard realist. The King who was shot dead as he was about to give a sermon telling us why America might go to hell. I hear the exiled, lonely philosopher Judith Shklar speaking back to the liberal fantasies of great men, reminding them that their ideas were stripped of moral purpose. I can hear Simone Weil say that only the forsaken know truth. I can hear my people: Pearl Gibbs, William Cooper, Charles Perkins, Marcia Langton. Each of these people who demanded justice as our birthright too. I hear my grandfather. I hear my language, a language Australia tried to silence.

I hear James Joyce and Czesław Miłosz. I hear Edward Said say that exile is a place of dwelling in space, an awareness that one is not at home. I hear Afua Hirsch, the Ghanaian British writer, say how she cannot pronounce her own name. Thirty-five years of living with that name, and still her tongue cannot quite find it. I hear her say that there are so many like her who have lost the sound of themselves, and given it over to others to tell them what their names are. Me too. I have a name and a sound to that name that I can never again recapture. I can learn again, but it will never be mine, purely, naturally mine. That is lost, buried under a blizzard of history. I hear Frantz Fanon say: 'Look, a negro!' That we are always being pointed at. I hear Albert Camus caution that every claim for justice is an invitation to hate.

The exiles. I hear them. In this moment, that's who I turn to. My soundtrack to the mourning for the dead White Queen. I hear Tom Waits, growling at me from the underbelly of America. Bob Marley's redemption song and love. Is this love that I'm feeling? He makes me feel like a sweepstakes winner. Aretha. Defiant Aretha; Aretha who blows down the walls of hope and demands respect. Sam Cooke, telling me a change is gonna come. Sometimes it sounds like Nusrat Fateh Ali Khan and the trill and thrill of my years in the backroads of Pakistan, watching people push against fear and violence. It is Tinariwen, rebel voices from Mali, bending blues out of shape. It is Amy Winehouse, saying we know she is no good, but I know she is beautiful. It is Johnny Cash, singing Soundgarden breaking his rusty cage to run. It is Archie Roach, whose voice could always pull down the stars from the sky. It is his wife and soul partner, Ruby Hunter, her voice a deep sorrowful and yet joyous moan to Archie's bruised tenor. These voices and so many more who have given melody and meaning to my wandering.

Exiles. They are all exiles. All cast adrift. Sometimes they have cast themselves adrift. They are running from the narrow confines of expectations. The exiles are swimming upstream from history. Some are lost. Some have lost a lot. Home for some will be a memory or a keepsake. But to me they have all gained something precious. They have second sight. They can see what others cannot. Theirs is the unconstructed conscience. They don't belong and so they embrace it. Black, White, borders – what are they? False. Constructed. As real as we make them. But exiles are not liberals. They are not from nowhere. They are not weightless. They are from somewhere and everywhere. They are a compass: one foot planted and one foot circling … forever circling.

I am an exile. I didn't choose exile but it chose me. I have followed it down every dirt road from my country to every far-off land I had dreamed of as a child. I have followed it far from home and far from family. And I cannot see what others want me to see. And that's good now. Especially right now.

These exiles demand of me honesty and truth. They know when I am lying and when I am pulling my punches. I know too those times when I have said things because I know it will be easier for people to hear. I know what they want to hear. That there is always the promise of redemption. There is a moral arc and it bends to justice. This is the poetry of Whiteness. They want to hear me talk about pain and sadness – just enough pain and sadness that they will cry. But their tears must be payment enough. They want to be absolved. I know this. And I have checked myself. I have told them that we should not apportion blame or guilt, and I see them heave with relief. And I take a bow to the sound of White applause. In that applause I hope I may have moved them. I hope that compromise is a fair price for convincing them. But I know that so many hearts are cold. Blame should be theirs. Guilt should be theirs. Right now I don't want to soften the blow.

Now the White Queen is dead.

When I hear that she has died, something breaks in me. It is not sadness that I feel. It is not shock. It is rage. And I am surprised at its intensity. I had thought – hoped – I had put this rage to rest. Made my peace with history, with the world. But now, hearing this news, it is immediate. I feel cheated. That the White Queen's death will now be mourned, while ours – the deaths of how many millions under the banner of empire – will be forgotten. I am consumed by fury. And it is personal. I am furious at the White Queen in a land far away, and I am furious at my own country. I am furious at people I call friends who are swept up in the myth of Whiteness.

And in my fury I am confronted again by the two consuming questions of my life: what is Whiteness? And what is it to live with catastrophe? From one comes the other. Within these questions are the dimensions of my existence. Whatever Whiteness is, it is not me. It was never meant for me.

Catastrophe is mine. I know what it is to come from a people whose existence on this Earth has not been assured.

Can I answer these questions without succumbing to hate? Can I slip the curse of vengeance, the vengeance that fires despots and murderers? Surely I know my people did not raise me for vengeance. Their gift to me was love. And I go in search of love. Love is not weakness. It is a furious love. And it is justice.

5

ELIZABETH

The White Queen is dead.

My mother's name is Elizabeth.

It is a name for a Queen. Like the White Queen, my mother might also be White. To most eyes, her skin is White – or at least what is called White. But to be White is to think yourself White, and for others – other people who think they are White – to consider you White as well. My mother has never been considered White. And she has never wanted to be.

My mother is consciously but not self-consciously Black. She has no need for grand gestures; she has nothing to prove. My mother has never needed to explain herself to the world. She lives her Blackness simply. I have never even asked her what her Blackness means. It has never occurred to me to ask.

Mum could not be anything other than what she is: the daughter of her parents, a product of her community, a sister and a mother, and all of it I know to be Black.

My mother could have taken a different path. She could have fled. Hidden out in the world of Whiteness. She could have lived a fraudulent life. God knows others have. She could have been like them and stashed away her family photographs and crossed the street to avoid her dark-skinned relatives. In time, she may have disappeared, erased every trace of her ancestry until even she believed her own lies. And I wouldn't blame her for it. So many saw an exit and ran. But who turns their backs on their blood? Who denies their own parents? What a cruel, cruel life that would be. But this is what Australia has asked of so many people; this was the price of admission to a society that was wilfully White.

Those dirty Blacks. That's what they called my mother and her family and all the beautiful people she lived among, laughed with, cried with, mourned with and loved with. There was in her little town, as in all little towns, a colour line. On one side the people who thought themselves White, and then the others – often of hue barely distinguishable from the White people themselves, and sometimes even with the same blood – who were the Blacks.

Those dirty Blacks. Blackness was a stain, an irremovable stain. To get close to it was to be stained as well. So it was for my grandmother Ivy, my mother's mother. Ivy was strikingly White. Blonde hair and alabaster skin, which she accentuated with White foundation and ruby-red lipstick. She was White like a 1920s Hollywood star. My mother said her mother's father was a German man, a big, old, straight-backed man named Joseph. I never knew him. I didn't know my grandmother's mother either, but I grew up believing she was a witch. A horrible old woman with a nasty streak who booted my grandmother out of home when Nan was still a girl.

My grandmother went to the nuns first. She tried to pass herself off as a Catholic and hoped they would take her in. In truth, she had barely set foot in a church. She told the nuns she was born in Bethlehem and baptised in the River Jordan. Her parents were Mary and Joseph, she said. The nuns sent her on her way, and that led her to a Black man in a tent by the river, who whistled at her as she walked by. In that tent with a man who was born under a tree in a place you can't find on a map and whose mother died when he was only a child, a little White girl found love, a love that in time would falter but never cease. That tent was a portal between worlds: Ivy passed from Whiteness into Blackness.

My grandmother mocked White civility and small-town manners. And she did it with rouge, high heels and tight skirts. What a battler. How subversive she was. Sexually subversive. Racially subversive. Her life was an outrage. She dared to live in the daylight what others hid in the darkness. There were plenty of sneaky White men preying on young Black girls at night and then ducking out before dawn. They left their mark in light-skinned kids raised without fathers. Everyone knew what was going on, but they kept their small-town secrets and went to their churches to pray for the sins of others. In 1930s Australia, Ivy was a sin, a White woman with a Black man, living among Black people and walking through town dolled up and laughing. Ivy was a crime.

Ivy used to say she was a White Aborigine. The man she loved was Black, her children were Black and her friends were Black. Her mother, after she had kicked Nan out of home, married a Black man herself, and my grandmother's brother was Black. My grandmother's White skin made her a target. White police made her life a misery. They would accuse her of running grog for the Blacks. They would upturn her pram carrying her babies, searching for alcohol she never had. The truth is my grandmother hated grog. If my grandfather was ever drinking, she would run and hide. He was the gentlest soul, my grandfather, and had never raised a hand to anyone. It was the grog Nan feared, not her man.

She would have done better to fear the White world. For in the eyes of White people, my grandmother had committed an unforgivable sin. The sin of love. Black love. And then she brought that love into the world. When she had gone into labour with her first child, she was turned away from the local hospital. She had eleven children, and two of them she buried far too young. She came to believe in our spirits. Among my people, the Willie Wagtail is a harbinger of death. One morning the tiny black-and-white bird danced at my grandmother's window, and she knew then that her sick little boy would not see out the day.

My grandmother lived, like all the other Black families, in a tin humpy – a one-room makeshift house built out of discarded kerosene tins and wrought iron – with a dirt floor. She would sweep the dirt clean with a brush made out of leaves and dampen the earth down with sprinkled water. The children slept under what they called a bag wagga – hessian bags stitched together. There was no running water. No heating. My grandmother cooked over an open fire. My grandfather worked at a Chinese market garden and would bring home fruit and vegetables that he supplemented with kangaroo and rabbit meat.

In a tin humpy, warmed with hessian bags and filled on kangaroo stew, my mother's family made a life. Here, with uncles and aunties and cousins all squeezed in alongside each other, they shared what they had. They told jokes and laughed and strummed guitars. I suspect these are things that White people do too. I don't really know because I didn't know White people. The people I was raised by were Black. They were family. I know how we ate and laughed and cried, and I know the songs we sang. Mournful old country songs mostly, songs about broken hearts, too much drinking, second chances, regret and hope. Some people might call it redneck music, but we turned them into Black songs of struggle and survival. We sang those songs to get through another day. And we sang with such freedom, such joy. That's the thing I remember most, the thing I am most grateful for.

We clung to our joy. I suspect we were always a joyous people. Look at our dance. Watch the way we move. Look at our art, daubed on our bodies. A people of misery don't emblazon themselves with such celebration. We wrote our stories on rocks and carved our ceremonies into trees. And when White people tried to crush that joy, we found it in each other. We suffered but, at least among the people I grew up with, we didn't bite down too hard on our bitterness. How I can see them now, with their heads tipped back and their mouths wide open and loud, loud voices rolling into each other and cackling, slapping their sides and laughing until tears came. I miss that. Whatever I may have gained in the world, it does not compare with our laughter, the sound of our love.

I don't deny that White people have joy. As I have grown, I have known them and I have felt their joy. I have even felt their love. I felt that love first from my White grandmother. A love with a hug from a White woman doused in baby powder and the smell of geraniums. A White woman cast adrift from White people. Whatever joy White people have, it was not enough to include my once-White grandmother. And that may be the difference between their joy and ours: ours is big enough to wrap its arms around anyone who needs it. Our joy always has enough to share.

My mother passed this joy to me. She passed it on in her defiance. Her grit. Her ability to stare down life. She passed it on in her stories. I grew up on stories of her childhood. How the Black women would gather together at the river to wash their clothes and dry them on the rocks while the kids played in the water. How she and her brothers and sisters would haul water in buckets up the hill from the river to their humpy home. How she and the other kids played cockatoo for the adults illegally playing cards. The cockatoo would perch in the tree and keep an eye out for the police. If the cops came, they would yell and the Black mothers and fathers would snatch their money and run, and whatever they spilled was pocketed by the fleet-footed Black kids.

My mother told me ghost stories. She lived in a world where there was no living, no dead. The dead spoke to Mum, appeared to Mum. She told me about the little man in the wheelchair she saw disappear before her eyes, and then weeks later she saw him again, lifted out of the back of a car by two old women in black dresses. She swears no one else saw him but her. She told me about a White man on a white horse who would sweep up behind her as she walked back across the open paddocks in darkness. A White man on a white horse – it's Biblical, isn't it? Torn from the pages of Revelations. *And I looked, and behold a pale horse; and his name that sat on him was Death, and Hell followed with him.*

I don't know if Mum ever read Revelations that closely. But she knew death. She knew that these stories – these ghost stories – would warn us. They would frighten us. The spirits marked the borders beyond which we could not pass. If we dared, a red-eyed, vicious, snarling dog would devour us. We were told ghost stories to warn us that someone was always watching us. And the ghosts Mum saw were White; they were always White.

Of course we are haunted. It makes such sense to me now. She was haunted, Mum. She was a haunted girl in a land that is haunted. It is haunted by what is lost. A deep ache that seems to come from the depths of the Earth.

Sit by a river at night and feel the rustle of wind and the hooting of owls and the stirring of animals and know that there is something else out there too. Not malevolent but mournful. At dawn, stand alone and watch the mist lift from the earth as it slowly warms under the rising sun. Watch how that mist fans out and spreads across an open field, like souls returning to rest. On crisp, cool mornings whenever I am back home, back on my land, I like to walk to the graveyard on the top of the hill and sit and feel the sunlight touching my face to open my ears to the sounds around me. There's a dog barking in the distance, and I see smoke from morning fires reminding me that there is life down there and it is stirring now.

All around me are headstones marking time and mortality. It reminds me just how random is this life and death. There's an old, chipped marker leaning into the earth; the names and dates are faded, worn away by wet winters and dry-bone summers. Here a child has lain in rest for over a hundred years. The child was loved and mourned once, but no one is left to mourn now. No one comes. No one lays flowers or rights the crooked gravestone. This is the fate of us all: to be forgotten and then to haunt the Earth.

I write about these ghosts because it helps explain some of the space between us. Between the world that Whiteness made and the world in which those of us who are Black dwell, there is a netherworld of spirits and haunting. I live in that haunting. That's one of my mother's gifts to me. The White blood in her veins could never strip the enchantment from her world.

The White world is devoid of magic. Magic is just a trick. Ghosts are tricks of the imagination. In place of magic is a cold rationality. That rationality, called science, created Whiteness itself, and the people who are White became their own gods. Science may unlock the secrets of the universe but also its destruction. Whiteness has already brought catastrophe. My people were exterminated. War and disease ravaged us. My mother and the people she lived among were the survivors. The ghosts my mother saw were the ghosts of empire.

❊

My mother's gift was her stories. The stories she told me as she stroked my forehead and sent me to sleep. And while we slept, my mother wrote. Writing was her refuge. Here she could return to her childhood, to the hills around her hometown, the river and the laughter and tears of those she loved. She wrote poems. Spare paeans to a time lost. Praise for those who saw her through. Joy and sadness. There are writers from the greatest schools, honoured in all the lands, who could not approach the aching, tender simplicity of my mother's words.

She wrote of the feared welfare men. Those child snatchers who would come to tear families apart.

The welfare's in town,
The welfare's in town.
They go to our homes
Don't knock just walk in

Show me the clothes for
The children
they'd say.

Where's the food?
What do they eat?

Show me the beds
Where are the sheets?

We'll report this
When the welfare board meets.

The welfare board took Mum's brothers and sisters. There in those welfare homes, they were broken. And they have never recovered. And this country told them it was good for them.

My mother wrote of her humpy home:

> … the dirt floors and double bed,
> Where five young children lay their heads.

And she wrote of the speckled fruit her mum used to buy. The rabbits they used to fry. And how broken biscuits made her cry.

6

LOOKING BACK

The White Queen is dead.

Words are what we are left with when everything else is taken. Stories, like genes, are passed down the generations. What fires someone to write? Surely it is to be heard. To speak into emptiness, into the darkness and the shadows; to speak into a chasm and hope that somewhere those words will echo. It is the same instinct to paint on a cave wall or to mark a tree; it says, *We were here. We mattered.* It speaks to the truth. My mother's words were a tear in a world of water. They were not written for anyone but herself and us. She was bearing witness to Whiteness. She was writing herself and those she loved into existence, because a White world had erased her.

Laws were written for people like my mother. Laws that excluded her. Laws that said although she may look little different to the White people she passed in the street, to them she was stained by Blackness. Australia wrote my mother in fractions. She and people like her – with what the state called 'an admixture of White blood' – were measured and weighed as Australia measured the weight of wool or wheat. Half-caste, quarter-caste, or octoroon: pieces of people divided according to how close to Whiteness they appeared. What was this country really saying? To be whole is to be White.

My mother was not the only writer in her family. Fossicking through some drawers at home when I was a young boy, I found a little green, hardcover book. It was an unpublished manuscript that my mother's brother, my uncle Kevin, had written; he called it *Looking Back*. He had gone to the trouble of having it bound and printed. I opened it and started to read.

I recognised the same gentle hand as my mother. The same effortlessness of style that can only come from someone who does not have to reach for imagination. Who writes with truth? Not truth for effect, just a truth that is what it is – that is true. And the truth of his little book broke my heart into a million pieces. I have never been able to put my heart back together. Because Uncle Kevin wrote about the person who more than any other I loved. He wrote about my grandfather.

Before I tell you what happened, let me tell you about my pa, Keith. He was the man who loved Ivy. If we knew nothing else about him but that, it would be enough. In loving Ivy, he defined himself. He was the Black man in a tent by the river who whistled at the pretty blonde girl as she walked by. He made room for her in his tent and made a place for her in his heart. He was a Kamilaroi man, a short, stout man who laughed easily, sometimes drank too much, read old western novels, loved a bet on the horses and loved me.

In my childhood I was closer to him than anyone else. My grandfather lived with us on and off. I would sit for hours with him, sometimes saying nothing, just feeling him close. We sat together listening to the radio each Saturday morning as horse-racing commentators ran through the form guide. My grandfather had his newspaper out and would mark his selections for the day. I would go with him as he put on his bets, then we would cheer his horses on and he would strike his leg with the rolled-up paper like a horse whip as he rode his winner home.

We would wait on the steps for the postman to come each pension day. If the mail was late, Pa would send me off to find the postman. I would run up and down the streets to fetch that pension cheque, because I knew what a day we would have. We had our own little ritual. Pa would cash his cheque and take me to the cafe for an ice cream with nuts and chocolate sauce in a glass bowl. Then he'd give me some money for my mother and head off to the pub. I would stay awake waiting for him to come home. I would hear him singing in the distance, then crashing into the side of our house. I would go out and help him in. Sometimes he'd scatter money over the ground and I would scoop it up and keep it. Days later, when he was skint, I would give it back to him. I took care of him and he took care of me.

That's why it was so hard to read what Uncle Kevin had written. He wrote about tragedy. About the time his little brother Neville died. He was only ten months old. All they had to bury him in was a little box. My uncle wrote how he and his sisters picked wildflowers and put them in the box with little Neville's white booties, and buried him in the ground next to the tin humpy they lived in. My uncle wrote about the time police came to that same block of land. They came to force Pa and his family to leave. A developer had bought it and the Blacks would be moved on. My uncle said the kids all ran away, his mother – my grandmother Ivy – was crying and Pa stood his ground. The police officer put his gun to my grandfather's head and my uncle said his father slumped to his knees. Then the bulldozer rolled over the home my grandfather had built.

Uncle Kevin tells this story better than I could.

'It was like we were part of that house too, and it was trying to help us somehow. But that big blade was too strong and the wire snapped and let go. Then our house came tumbling down and lay motionless in the dust. It was all over in a few seconds.'

✳

The White Queen is dead.

My grandparents' love defied a country and it defied an idea – an idea of Whiteness. Was my grandmother White? To those White police, she wasn't. She wasn't White to the Black man she loved, the Black children she brought in to the world or the Black people who opened their arms to her. My grandmother was no longer White to White people, and that's why they broke her. They broke her by treating her as Black. Or maybe something worse, she was someone who chose to be Black. Love made her Black … for a while. Just a while.

The life Ivy shared with my grandfather couldn't last. She left and she married another man. She told my mother that she was out of her mind. She said she had a breakdown, and when she came to her senses she was with a man she did not love, and far from her children and the little tin humpy and her Keith. She never stopped loving Keith. Sometimes they would run away together. For a few weeks they would be the kids who shared a tent by the river. Their love never ended, she said. She carried his photo forever. But there was too much pain. They could be strong in those broken places, but not strong enough together. My grandmother would go back to a loveless place – to a good man, but not her man. She would go back to Australia, crossing that racial threshold that divided us then and divides us still. Australia, the place that rejected her, was also her escape.

With her White skin, ruby lips and curly blonde hair, my grandmother, to those who passed by her, was now just another old White lady. She was no longer a threat. No longer a scandal. No more did the police stop her in the street. She was welcome at the hospitals that had turned her away when she was having her child. She was back, and the lie of Whiteness could again become her lie.

Yes, I suppose this is the truth: that as much as she was my blood, my grandmother was ultimately White. Even if there remained a part of her that did not belong to White Australia, White Australia belonged to her. She could possess it. And that's what Whiteness is, after all: it is possession. Possession of land, possession of souls.

My grandmother's Whiteness gave her a choice that was never available to her Keith, to her children or to me. I have asked myself: *Is this betrayal?* Yes, I suppose it is, as harsh as that sounds. Even those White people we love can betray us. I have friends who have betrayed me, who have laughed at the racist joke, who have kept quiet when they should have spoken up. Every day without justice for what Whiteness has inflicted on people who are not White is a betrayal. Whiteness itself betrays our shared humanity. White people created a place for themselves above others. They created the world and we were bludgeoned into it. My White grandmother – for now she was White again – crossed that border from our world to hers. She crossed the border into a world where the White Queen reigned.

My grandfather never loved again. Not like that. He never had a home again. His home lay crushed under a bulldozer. He never returned to the grave of little Neville, buried in that box that my grandfather had made for his dead boy. Little Neville lived – I have to remind myself of that. His death doesn't tell all of his story. Neville smiled, gurgled, clasped his father's hand in the way that babies do. He hugged and slept on his father's chest. For ten months he lived, his eyes each day taking in more and more of our wondrous world. Neville – that's his name. By ten months he would have known that name. He would have recognised the sounds of voices and the faces of those who loved him. He never knew he was not White. He was saved from that brutal reckoning. But he is lost, buried somewhere with nothing to mark his grave. Buried, like countless other Black lives whose names we do not know, under the weight of Australia.

This is why my mother writes. It is why my Uncle Kevin bound and printed his own little book. They didn't write thinking anyone would read their words. They wrote because those things needed to be said. They wrote because those words needed to live in the world. They wrote about broken biscuits and wire, because those things were them. The broken biscuits Mum cried over were the shattered lives she saw around her. The broken piece inside her. That wire that held on so tight to that little tin humpy is Uncle Kevin, who held on to his memories.

That little green book lay in my mother's drawer and I found it. That book is my voice – not a voice I need to ask Australians to give me, to vote on. It is the voice that comes from my blood, and more than the Constitution – more than the laws of our parliaments, more than an anthem – more than all the songs and films and novels that purport to tell the story of us here in this land, Uncle Kevin's book told me what I had to know about this place called Australia.

❊

The White Queen is dead.

My thoughts are not with her or her family. My thoughts are with my own family. My thoughts are with my grandfather, the person I loved as deeply as I could love anyone, and how police the colour of the White Queen and wearing the White Queen's insignia aimed at a gun at him and brought him to his knees. I don't want to hear about the White Queen's devotion to duty, because her police did their duty and bulldozed my mother's home. I won't waste a minute mourning the loss of the White Queen – I will mourn an uncle I never knew, buried I know not where. I will mourn little lost Neville, with his white booties and flowers picked by my mother and her brother, whose resting place was defiled by the White Queen's police.

Damn Australia. Damn it to hell for what it did to my family, what it did to countless Black families, Black families with White blood more often than not, but families who could never be White. Damn the White Queen too. That's what I want to say when I hear she had died. Let's not forget there is no Australia without her. Her crown is the Crown that stole this country – it is the Crown that smashed Black lives. These things were done in her name. Let's not forget, too, that in her time, during her reign, the crimes against us continued.

The dispossession did not end in the eighteenth or nineteenth centuries. It continued into the twentieth century.

This country was not done with stealing our land. In the year that I was born, 1963, police wearing the White Queen's insignia in a place we call Queensland set fire to the homes of Aboriginal people to force them out and claim their land. The White Queen, far away on her throne, said nothing. That is her duty. To the servants of the White Queen, those people meant nothing. They were in the way of the expansion of White Australia. Those people from Mapoon have never forgotten. They remember that night as 'The Burning'.

They were just like my grandfather and his family. They meant nothing either to the Crown that valued rights as long as you were White. Australia has had laws defending and protecting White rights over others. While this nation wrote laws defending private property, it saw no contradiction taking away ours. Why would it? This nation was built on extinguishing our rights. We forget this far too readily. We are conditioned to forget it. The forgetting starts in school, when we lay White history over Black. The forgetting bends time and space until the original sin recedes and appears as a dot on the horizon. Then the White Queen dies and is mourned, as those who have lived and died under the heaving weight of the Crown are forgotten.

So we must remember. This nation sent people to war on the other side of the world, wars against tyranny, yet this nation had no problem inflicting tyranny on us here. This nation has memorials to those wars, yet our wars – wars that killed more people than any of those wars – are forgotten. Fate did not put my grandfather, my grandmother, my mother and my uncle at the mercy of the state. The state did that. The state that bears the seal of the Crown. This state that valued White lives above Black. This state decided who was White, and cast out my grandmother, turned her away from hospital, terrorised her in the street and crushed the grave of her dead child.

Why wouldn't I damn them all? This Australia, born out of theft and slaughter and built on a law to keep the country White, which still today does not formally recognise the First Peoples, which has signed no treaties – how does this country hold its head high in the world? That's the question I ask. And the answer, to me, is that it is shameless. It is a place beyond shame. Why would I think otherwise? Yes, damn it all. And I admit to satisfaction in that resentment. In my anger I know I am right.

But there's something else in me. There is love. There is the love of a people who truly know what love means. Whose love has been tested and found inexhaustible. And that love saved me. And I know that love is not love if it is only reserved for those who love us.

So I will love them, those who were without love for us. And I will not damn Australia. I will not damn the White

Queen to hell. I won't surrender to them the love my people put in me. That is not our way and that is not who I am. I will give them my love. Damnation is not strong enough anyway. Better pity.

Yes, I will pity her and I will pity them. I pity that they can be so inhumane. I pity their ignorance and their arrogance. I pity a people who believe in their own lies. I pity their power and how it has twisted them so. I pity the people kneeling now before the dead White Queen. I pity the White Queen and all the silliness that surrounds her. And I pity all of this Whiteness. And most of all I pity that they love it so.

7

WHY ARE YOU SO BLACK?

The White Queen is dead.

'I honour my God. I serve my Queen. I salute the flag.'

Funny the things that linger. My earliest memory of school is not my mother dropping me off in tears at the gate. It isn't playing with my friends. It isn't running to the canteen at recess. It is this, a pledge to a queen and a flag that was never mine. That could never be mine.

The indoctrination started early. A little Aboriginal boy, the darkest face in his all-White class, standing to attention at the school assembly and pledging allegiance to the White Queen. I can see myself wearing someone else's cast-off clothes, shy and with a sad smile I always wore that covered how scared I really was. I knew I was not like the other kids.

They were loud and confident, never doubting that the world was made for them. I was always hoping no one would notice me. I wanted to shrink from it all.

This was 1960s Australia, a nation White by law. A nation that told itself stories of settlers and explorers and convicts, all White. A nation where the fleece of sheep was prized more than the lives of Aboriginal people. It was a nation of *Pick a Box, Bellbird, This Day Tonight*; television ads for Palmolive soap, Holden cars and Chiko Rolls; and bronzed surfers. It was a world that didn't include us. This was the lucky country and we were poor, bugger me.

It seems now like such a cruel, cruel trick to play on a child. What nation is this that strips everything from a people, then tells their children to bend a knee? I knew that this was not right. Even at the age of five or six, I knew this was not me. I told my grandfather, the man who had lost his home to White police, that my school wanted me to pledge allegiance to that same crown. He told me to put my fingers behind my back, and while I could say the words I wouldn't mean it. That was my little childhood protest. Even today, when the anthem plays, I can't sing. When I look at the flag and I see the symbol of Britain in the corner, I am reminded of what this country truly believes.

In that same school, I was taught about race and racism. I learned what it was to be White, and I learned that whatever

White was, I was not it. Like the pledge to Whiteness in the school assembly, I was confronted by a terrifying idea of what Whiteness means. It was another young boy who told me what my place in the world was: that by virtue of his birth, he was somewhere above me. He could ask me whatever he wished, turn me into an object, or demand of me to justify my existence, to explain myself. What's more, this boy would not have thought for a minute that anything he was doing was wrong. He would not have thought for a minute that he did not have the right. Because he was White, and these people think that White is always right.

If I close my eyes, I am back there. We are sitting on the floor in our classroom. The teacher is reading from some book or other – I don't remember what it was, but I remember exactly what the White boy next to me said. I remember what he looked like. In White 1960s Australia, he was the Whitest White boy. It was as though he had stepped from a Milky Bar Kid chocolate commercial. You may recall it: a blond, freckle-faced boy with a six-shooter on his hip and a cowboy hat. Whiteness personified. Whiteness packing a gun. Whiteness and violence dreamed up in an advertising agency to sell a chocolate bar. The Milky Bar Kid put his arm next to mine. With a smile he asked, 'Why are you so Black?'

I am sure it was the first time I had been asked that question. Black? I lived among people I loved. I lived among people of laughter and tears and music. I lived among people who loved sport. They watched the same television programs that other people watched. These people – my people – swam in the rivers and loved an open fire. They did these things as people do. But other people made them Black – or, rather, these other people made themselves White. Now I was being confronted by their reality that someone, just another boy in so many ways just like me, could set me apart. Because he was White, he could ask me why I was so Black.

I can't tell you how I answered. I probably smiled awkwardly and lowered my eyes. The question is what matters, and from that day I have never stopped trying to find an answer.

The evils of the world spill forth at these moments. From this time on, I could never forget what I knew. From that day forward I would be Black. My life was framed in that one question: *Why are you so Black?* This boy never thought to ask himself why he was so White. Why would he? Our teacher was White, the other children in the class were White, the people who worked in the shops we stopped in on the way home were White, and the people on those television shows we watched were White. Whiteness was normal. Whiteness was power.

And this boy never had to question his power. He was born into it. He was born White. No questions necessary. He had power over me, this White boy, a power to tell me that I was not like him and that he was better than me.

Some may dismiss this as childhood curiosity. Just another boy wondering why I looked different to him. I have thought about that myself. I have wondered if I am reading too much into this. But then I ask: *Why has this moment stayed with me?* Above all the memories of childhood, why does this one – just like being asked to bow to the White Queen – stay with me? It is too easy to dismiss this. That's how racism works: it orders the world. It tells us what matters and what doesn't. It convinces us that racism is all in our heads. And if we listen to that, we are lost. We have surrendered to racism. We have accepted its logic. We have accepted that they are always innocent. That boy was not innocent: he was the product of the world his ancestors made. He was born into their sin, yet he knew – in that question he asked, which some may see as so benign – that there was nothing I could do about it.

I recall how this moment made me feel. I was reeling. My world had been upturned. My footing was no longer sure. There was another Aboriginal boy in my year – but in another class – and I told him what had happened. My friend was the adopted son of the White Presbyterian minister and his wife.

They had adopted six Black kids. Kids who were not being raised by their own; who were not growing up in their culture. He lived right behind me, but between his fence and mine there was a space as big as this nation itself. I envied him. I would go to his house with running water and heating and beds with clean sheets and a full fridge. To me, he lived in a dream. When I looked at him, I felt ashamed of what we were.

That day when I told him about the Milky Bar Kid, we rushed from school back to his home. I recall now how his mother greeted us at the door. She was a big, open-hearted woman, and when I think of her I think of her kitchen and the smell of warm cake. My friend told her that someone had asked why I was so Black. He needed to know from his mother: 'Are we Black?'

I think of what she could have said. She could have told us that, yes, we were Black and that this was our land, and we came from a culture that was rich and deep, and that our people had survived and that was a miracle.

She could have said all of those things, and she would have been speaking the truth. But she did not; her answer was the answer I would come to hear so often from White people. We became the problem. Not him – not the boy whose Whiteness gave him power over who I was. We were the problem.

'You're not Black,' she said. 'You have lovely olive skin.'

And there it was. So sweet. So caring. She wanted to protect us from the world. She wanted to just hold the ugliness of racism at bay for another day. But she was racist herself. There's no other word for it. Here was a lesson for me: racism can have the kindest face.

In her own gentle way, she told us that to be Black was something to deny. She told us that there was something wrong with being Black. She did not for one minute question herself. She was born into Whiteness, with all of its certainty. She was raising Black kids in a home of warmth and love. Of Sunday dinners in front of the television watching *Disneyland*. This was her own fantasy. She wrapped her big arms around these little Aboriginal kids that she called her own, she looked at me too with love, and yet for all that, in her Whiteness she could not see us.

In one day I had been asked why I was so Black and then been told that I wasn't Black at all. In this loving White woman's answer lay the truth for me and my friend. Whatever we were, we were most assuredly not White.

I am not alone in these memories. I have spoken to other Black people who had their own childhood reckoning with race. They tell me it happened in the same place. It happened at school. Of course it did. This is where the world grabs hold of us. This is where our minds are shaped. My horizons were set by a White boy, the son of White parents in a White country. I was inducted into the glorious world of Whiteness; I learned about their heroes, their myths, their poets, their politicians. And I remember – as all Black kids remember – that none of these heroes looked like me.

Other Black kids have told me of feeling ashamed, just as I did. I know they share the scars of that childhood. I know they share another memory of mine: how as a boy I sat in a bath rubbing my skin red-raw, trying to rub off the Blackness. I wanted to be White; I wanted to be like the Milky Bar Kid.

8

THE INVENTION OF
WHITENESS

The White Queen is dead.

The latest White monarch in a land where only White people have sat on that throne. In her land, under the rule of her ancestors, Whiteness was born. No, invented. Because Whiteness is an invention. It was created to crush other people. Whiteness made the world, a world it dominated by force, and then it made its domination legal. It wrote laws that underwrote the theft of other people's land. It wrote laws that put chains around the necks of Black people and put them to work to make untold riches for White people. The great, destructive power of Whiteness was to decide who was White. It divided up the world and placed Whiteness at the top.

Whiteness set the borders of our world and the borders of our imaginations.

Some books have such force that they are like the power of nature itself. Words and ideas can reorder the world. In these moments, the heavens can break open and I can glimpse eternity. I can see to the beginning of time itself.

That's what it felt like when I picked up Theodore W. Allen's *The Invention of the White Race*. It took a White man from the United States, a nation built on genocide and slavery, to reveal that Whiteness is not just a social construct, but a power construct; and that while it is not 'real', as there is no biological basis to race, it is at the same time all too real. Others like African-American historian Nell Irvin Painter – herself influenced by Allen – who revealed to her country the original sin of its Whiteness; and in Australia Black women like Marcia Langton, Jackie Huggins, Megan Davis, Larissa Behrendt, Aileen Moreton-Robinson, Anne Patel-Gray, Sue Green – have helped light my path. They speak back to law, politics, and faith. They have refused to accept the lie of Whiteness.

Whiteness defined the space between the barbarous and the civilised. It was a trap. Human beings – real, living, breathing human beings of blood and bone and soul – were deemed uncivilised and therefore not White. If they resisted the oppression of Whiteness, then that would prove they were unworthy to be ranked among the civilised at all. Submit or die. Look around the world and trace White footprints and you will follow the trail of tears.

If I told you about land stolen, about language silenced, about faith erased, about slaughter; if I told you about children snatched from their families and 'trained' to be 'White', where would your mind go? It sounds so awfully familiar, doesn't it? It is a story that has played out from the Americas to Africa to Australia, but these evils were conceived, practised and perfected in Ireland. That's what Theodore W. Allen reveals. Ireland in the imagination today may appear to be a White country. It wasn't always so. Allen tells us that in Ireland, race was fixed as a social category, and racial slavery was fixed as a system of social control.

From the thirteenth century, when the Anglo-Normans took control, the indigenous Gaelic Irish were marked by race. They were not seen as equal in law. Irish tribal kinship, which defined communal property, was tossed aside and land was plundered. An Irish person was not considered fully human. In 1278, two Anglo-Norman men were charged with rape but found not guilty because the victim was 'an Irish woman'. By the seventeenth century, Allen tells us, 'the Irish were regarded by English law as foreigners in their own land'. Under English law they had no defence against the brutality wreaked upon them.

During the Protestant ascendancy, the Irish were considered a 'barbarous' people. As in America, where the term *Negro* means 'slave', the term *Hibernicus* – Latin for 'Irishman' – was, Allen says, the legal term for 'unfree'. In the US state of Georgia the killing of a 'Negro' was not a felony, similarly in Ireland Anglo-Norman priests granted absolution to murderers because it was no more a sin to kill an Irishman than it was to kill a dog.

In Ireland the British embarked on a program of complete conquest. Force and famine – which took hundreds of thousands of lives – brought the Irish to their knees. After the Irish rebellion was quashed in the mid-seventeenth century, thousands of Irish soldiers were sold to foreign nations. Hundreds of women and children were sold as bond labourers to America. This is what is known as the Irish slave trade.

The Protestant English wanted to sever the ties of Irish families to their Catholic faith. The most vulnerable became targets: take the children and break a culture. Under a system of charter schools, Catholic children were removed from their families, as Allen says, becoming 'inmates' of state, never to be released until they were adults. They were held far from their family homes and raised in ignorance of their faith, of their culture, even of their very names. What was tried in Ireland was exported to the 'boarding' schools of America, where

'Indian' children were taken: their long hair was cut, they were given Western clothes to wear – stiff collars and tight-fitting coats – and they were forbidden from speaking their languages. In Australia we are still learning about the pain of our 'stolen generations', Aboriginal children put in dormitories and welfare homes, so often abused, and farmed out to work for White families. These were people like my great-aunt, who was stolen from her family and raised apart from her brothers and sisters; she slept under a sign that said: 'Think White, act White, be White'.

Now, here's the thing I have come to know: Whiteness is not about colour. It is not about White people. The Irish, to our modern eyes – bludgeoned as we have been to see the world through colour – are demonstrably White. But this is about people who *think* they are White. The English invented Whiteness and they prosecuted it. The Irish, to the British conquerors, were Black, barbarian. The politics of Ireland were the politics of race. The British imposed a racial order. Racial oppression became entrenched racial superiority.

The Irish resistance intensified. It was draining British resources, troops and treasure. By the mid-eighteenth century, the British switched from a policy of racial oppression to national oppression. As they would do in other parts of the world, in Ireland they chose to divide and conquer. They would use the Irish against the Irish. Laws had started to change, loosening controls on Irish land ownership. A wealthier class of Irish emerged. How could they be incorporated into the British racial power structure without upsetting the Protestant order or inspiring a move for independence? The Irish were drafted into the garrison enforcing British rule. They became agents in their own oppression.

My family is tied to this history. As surely as the British imposed a racial order here on my Aboriginal ancestors, they did so too against my Irish forebears. My great-great-grandfather, John Grant, joined the Irish resistance. He and his brother were United Irishmen. His sister and his mother were part of the struggle. They conspired in the death of a British landlord's son and were executed. John, aged only seventeen, was transported to the colony of what would become Australia. He was banished for life, never to see Ireland again. He had children with a Wiradjuri woman, Gurrawin, and I carry their blood today. I am born of the idea of Whiteness. This lie made truth – biological nonsense weaponised into violent power – has shaped my entire life.

I have never escaped its clutches. When I think I may have slipped free of race, it returns, spitting at me. The people who think they are White know the power it gives them and they know they can use it with vicious effect. They know how to hurt us. Like the time I was standing out the back of the ABC studios in the centre of Sydney, filming with a cameraman. He is Chinese and knows too how race can define the contours of world. Inside the ABC I hold a position of responsibility, of privilege, some might even imagine of power. I broadcast to and write for an audience potentially of millions. My face is familiar enough that I am recognised and often stopped in the street. Almost everyone I meet is courteous, friendly; many are supportive. When I meet them, I like to imagine that this is my country, that Australia is mine too. Then I see another face.

We know racism. We can sniff it in the air. We can sense its threat even before it arrives. On this day I could feel what was coming. I was recording directly to camera, and I saw out of the corner of my eye a young man and his girlfriend walking towards me. He got close enough that I could have reached out and touched him, and then he said it. He unleashed that word that I have never truly learned to speak back to. He spoke it loudly, so that all could hear. 'Nigger,' he said.

For a moment I was breathless. I was dizzy. My cameraman looked at me, hurt and confused. Then I felt rage rising in my chest. I turned. 'What did you say?' I yelled. The man's girlfriend gripped his arm and steered him away; I felt that she was embarrassed. My cameraman tried to calm me, to tell me not to worry about it. I think he just wanted to get out of there.

There was no way for me to process that moment. Nothing could make sense of it. Is this what I was, a 'nigger'? I tried to tell myself that this man was just a fool. I reassured myself that of the hundreds of people I might have walked past that day, only this one had made that comment. Yes, that is true. But that word makes all the difference. It erases everything else. Why? Because it lands with the power of history. That word marked the world between that man and me. Even those people who would offer kindness and respect, even those who would be appalled at what he had said, they were White too, and they were part of that world that gave that horrible word its power. They were formed out of that world where that word meant people would bear the scars from whippings, where chains would be placed around their bodies, where people would hang from trees. That word kills people still. This was their world, and in that moment that poisonous man reminded me that their world was not mine, could never be mine. That man reminded me that I could not trust White people, and if I do, I can get hurt. He stole my trust in even those I love.

I felt weak and I felt ashamed that day. For all I might have accomplished in the world, that one word had reduced me to that scared little boy being asked, 'Why are you so Black?' Who was that young man? I will never know. It doesn't matter, either – what matters is that he was White, and he thought that gave him power over me. He could inflict violence on me.

For the rest of that day, I felt as if the world was just slightly out of sync. Whatever else I did, I could never get back the seconds that it took for that man to say that word.

I left work that night and got in my car to drive home, and there, alone with my thoughts, I cried.

9

WHAT COLOUR WILL HER CHILDREN BE?

The White Queen is dead.

In her own family, a Black woman has been cast adrift. Forced out. Blamed for lowering the tone of the royals. For not doing her duty. For taking a White Prince and leading him astray. This Black woman is the temptress. She has cast a spell. But the truth is she is the one hexed. The spell is Whiteness and she has eaten of the poisoned apple.

I have never met Meghan Markle. But I know her. And she knows me. If I pass another person on the street – a person not White – there is a nod between us. A look in each other's eye that says, *I see you*. The tears that I have cried are the tears millions of others have cried. They are the same tears Meghan Markle has shed.

What race is Meghan Markle? The world has seemed obsessed with this question. When Meghan, a young American actress, met and fell in love with Prince Harry, the White Queen's grandson, she began to understand, she said, what it was like to be treated as a 'Black woman'. Until then, she said, she had been treated 'as a mixed woman'. Now she became more definitively 'Black'. Yes, she had experienced racism before, but this was different. Meghan had lived her life, she said, 'in-between worlds': White and Black. It was a dreamlike state, a fiction between two fictions. Meghan was living a lie.

Meghan was trapped in a world of race and racism. She could not begin to describe herself without accepting the awful logic of race. What does it mean to be mixed? It means that we are different species. That, like cattle, we can be interbred. By describing herself as 'mixed', Meghan Markle was living out her own confusion. Two parts of herself tearing at the one soul. At one time White. At the other Black. And always somewhere in between.

We tie ourselves in knots trying to explain ourselves to an uncomprehending world. The American census now asks people to self-identify in ever more convoluted and exotic abstractions and hyphens. The golfer Tiger Woods has gone to ludicrous linguistic lengths to describe himself, inventing his own category, 'Cablinasian', to reflect his Caucasian, Black, Indian and Asian roots. Meghan Markle herself, in an op-ed for *Elle* magazine, wrote of how she has embraced 'the gray area surrounding my self-identification, keeping me with a foot on both sides of the fence'.

But as both Tiger and Meghan have discovered to their cost, there is only the bluest eye, and that eye sees all. Meghan Markle had entered the very realm of Whiteness to discover that there was nothing 'mixed' about her. She was Black. She was discovering now what that meant.

For a while Meghan was a novelty. An American actress. A new celebrity to adorn magazines. There may even have been something exotic about her. But it turned. And the criticism was more than tinged with racism. Listen to the commentary: she didn't 'look royal', she was not as graceful as Prince William's White wife, Kate. She was portrayed as a wrecker, an opportunist, a gold-digger, someone leading Harry astray. Trolls called her son the N-word. She was criticised for the clothes she wore, the food she ate, and the colour of her nail polish. All of it was another way of asking the question I had been asked as a boy, the question so many of us face: *Why are you so Black?*

Why did media and commentators so dislike Meghan? They surely didn't know her. But they did know one thing about her – and to them it was the essential thing: she was not White. And they loathed her for that. So much did they loathe her that they came to loathe Harry. The Prince was seen as hapless. He had fallen under the sway of a temptress. Kate Middleton brought a rosy English glow to William. But Meghan darkened the royals' door. Prince Harry had been reckless and offensive in the past. He had dressed in Nazi costume with a swastika on his sleeve. Yet that never stopped him from being hailed, at one point, as Britain's favourite royal. Yes, they preferred Harry as a racist than Harry married to a Black woman. Is it any wonder this broke Meghan? It breaks us all. She and Harry fled the royal household. They are no longer 'royals'. It was that or kill herself. That's what Meghan was driven to. She told Harry she didn't want to live anymore.

Yes, for the first time in her life, Meghan Markle began to understand what it was to be a Black woman.

❉

Race is a strange subject. It is an utterly discredited notion; scientists know this. They know it is nonsense to even speak of 'race'. We belong to one human family, and advances in the study of DNA show that we all draw our heritage from different parts of the globe. In this way, we are all 'mixed'. The geneticist David Reich says 'the genome revolution – turbocharged by ancient DNA – has revealed that human populations are related to each other in ways that no one expects'. According to him, 'if we trace back our lineages far enough into the past, we reach a point where everyone descends from the same ancestor'. The evidence of human remains tells us that ancestral 'Eve' was from Africa.

Yes, the Queen is African, and Harry and Meghan – like the rest of us – are distant cousins.

Meghan Markle was no more 'mixed race' than anyone else at her wedding. But that is the only way she could understand herself. The only way she could render herself comprehensible to a world that asks over and over and over: *Why are you so Black?* Scientifically, race is rubbish, yet it matters. It matters because, as a society, we have made it matter. Ideas of 'race' have brought out the worst in humanity. They have inspired – and continue to inspire – genocide, holocaust, war, dispossession, colonisation, imperialism, slavery, lynching, segregation, and mass incarceration.

Personally and individually, race ties us in knots. Meghan's mother is considered Black and her father White. Had Meghan lived slightly earlier, America's 'one-drop rule' – one drop of Black blood – would have meant she was Black. She could have been bought and sold. Her body could have been violated. She could have been shut out of diners and cinemas. She would have to have ridden at the back of the bus. She would have to have dropped her eyes when a White person walked by. She would have to have answered 'No, sir' and 'Yes, ma'am'. All of this because of a fiction dreamed up by mad race scientists and so-called enlightened philosophers, who looked upon the world and saw not a shared humanity, but bodies to be owned. Land to be conquered. They saw themselves in the image of God, and the rest of us as primitive souls to save.

Race has us trapped. It is all but impossible for us to think about ourselves or articulate a sense of identity without referring to race. What am I? I have deep Indigenous heritage through my mother's and my father's families. Historically, we have been categorised as 'Aboriginal' or 'Indigenous' – or, more colloquially or disparagingly, as 'Blacks'. That has meant, at various times, being subject to government policies that have restricted our liberty, and told us where we could live and who we could marry.

Families have been divided on arbitrary rulings of colour. The Australian Law Reform Commission lists more than sixty different historical definitions of who we are. Who is considered Black? All the names they have had for us. Aborigines, Aboriginals, Indigenous. Never who we were.

Always what they saw. Today, I am asked to tick a box on the census form identifying whether I am Aboriginal.

I am descended from Wiradjuri and Kamilaroi people, but I also have an Irish convict ancestor and my maternal grandmother was European. How can that census box possibly contain all of me?

I am asked to 'identify' as Aboriginal. And I don't trust identity any more than I trust race. I *am* a Wiradjuri, Kamilaroi and Dharrawal person. I *am* – if you must use these words – Aboriginal, Indigenous. I don't *identify*, I *am*. Identity? It is something to possess. It begins with the letter I. The building block of modernity. 'I' the individual was supposed to set us free. But it made everything optional. Everything becomes a choice. There are people who choose to identify as Aboriginal. People who can trace the faintest lineage. And that's okay. If they find pride in that, that's okay. But I have no need of it.

Let me tell you about identity. Identity is the pathway to tyranny. Identity leads to the gulag and the gas chamber. This is the worst of identity. The identity that sets fire to our world. What the Indian philosopher and Nobel laureate economist Amartya Sen called 'solitarist identities'. These things that divide us, that shrink us, that demand we choose our sides. And so we do. And we tear ourselves limb from limb. As a reporter, I have seen these wars. The bloodied marketplaces. The sacrifice of innocents.

Sen is right: identity kills. It kills with abandon. Hindu against Muslim, Catholic against Protestant, Hutu against Tutsi, Shia against Sunni. How I could go on and on. All of the stories I have told. And I recoil from ideas of identity. I don't like the word – I don't like what it conjures. I don't like the modern manifestation of that word, which so easily leads to tribalism. To an idea that we are defined not by who we are, but who we are not, or what we are not.

It is one of the hallmarks of this modern age: to marry the quest for identity – to belong somewhere – with grievance, especially historical grievance. Here lie the fault lines of our world. The philosopher Hegel – the great thinker of the idea of history – saw us on a highway of despair. And I think that's the journey I am on. A journey on that highway of despair. My journey through the world, through my own history, my family's history. Grappling with the legacy of that, the resentment that that history can bring, and yet wanting to be free of the chains of that history, to have a place of belonging, but not a place of permanent identity. I want to interrogate those ideas of race, Blackness, Whiteness – all of these things that put us into boxes.

I want to think myself free. I want to know if I can live with history without being chained to history. When I speak of the wounds of history, it is to open them to sunlight, not to bathe them in salt.

History can be the poison in the blood of our identities. It is so tempting and seductive to identify myself with the historical wound. Nietzsche talked about people being consumed by a historical fever; he called it *ressentiment*. That desire to return forever to the wound. The wound that is the source of identity – identity, but not freedom. To Nietzsche, it is a tyranny of the weak. True – it can be. And yet, at the same time, I know that the wound has shaped me. I am a product of invasion, colonisation, and empire. It still affects the lives of people in my family. It is in my bones. It is in my blood. It is, you know, my mother's milk, what I was raised on: those stories of never forgetting what happened to us.

So I grapple with the liberal impulse to park history, to leave history in the past. To forgive, or even better to forget – that is the liberal project. Even as I know – I know all too well – that to drink from the toxic well of history can lead us to violence. I struggle with those impulses, with the history that is so alive; I struggle with wanting to forgive and forget, because it feels like letting people off the hook.

Where is freedom on the highway of despair? To forgive may be noble; holy, even. Yet *ressentiment* feels righteous. So I live somewhere between resentment and forgiveness, between hope and hopelessness. Here I am clinging on to the past yet also wanting to look to the future, having progress, being a part of modernity, which promises to set me free – from faith, traditions, even our families. Yet there is nothing to hold on to in that freedom. There is the promise of release, yes. Yet without my history I am lost in the world. And so I hover in that space in between – to paraphrase Eliot, holding the fragments together that I shore against my ruin.

I turn my face to freedom. I turn to the past to point me to the future. I turn my face to justice. But I have no need of identity, which shrinks my world, which turns me to the face of Medusa, which turns me to stone.

✽

The White Queen is dead.

Can I think myself free of identity? More than that, can I even begin to speak of myself as free of race? I don't mean race blindness; I don't trust those people who say they don't see colour. That itself erases us. I want to be seen. What I don't want is to be defined by what you see.

Can we be truly post-racial? That's what so many want to believe. Like millions around the world, I watched Barack Obama being sworn in as the American president. The first

Black president. I remember how White commentators seized on this as a moment of liberation. But it was theirs, not ours. They were now free of the stain of slavery. They were now free of race. They recited Martin Luther King, how people should be judged by the content of their character, not the colour of their skin. White people love that idea. But they rarely look to the colour of their own skin. It is always us – those who are not White – they believe King was talking to. They also forget that King was dreaming.

I heard these White commentators tell Black people: no more excuses. Obama was proof that Black people could achieve anything. As if racism is just an excuse. As if the problem is us. This is the logic of race, of racism. It is always our problem. I am reminded of this as I watch a television report of yet another massacre in America. A crazed White man with a gun has shot dead Black people in a supermarket. The reporter is trying to sound sympathetic but cannot escape her own racism. Racism she is not even conscious of. The Black people were murdered, she says, because of the colour of their skin. No, they weren't. There is nothing in the colour of their skin that should mean they are gunned down in broad daylight. Their skin has nothing to do with it. They were killed because of what the crazed White man with a gun *believed* about Black skin.

That's the twisted logic of racism: that racism is never what others do. It is what we feel, we are told. What we experience. It is what we suffer. Here's the truth: racism created the idea of race. Not the other way around. And Whiteness always absolves itself. Yes, racism is abhorrent. But it is never the fault of Whiteness. It is never inherent to Whiteness. It is something inherent to us. It is about the colour of our skin. That's why we are killed. It is never about the colour of White skin. The television reporter could have said that a dozen Black people were killed because of the colour of the crazed White gunman's skin. But that would never have occurred to her. She is White, and Whiteness orders our world.

The historian Barbara J. Fields and her sister, sociologist Karen E. Fields, have coined a word for this: *racecraft*. Race is like sorcery, they say. Its power comes from our willingness to believe in it. It is witchcraft. The crops in the field have died; it must be the fault of witches. The Fields sisters trace the prevalence of magic and superstition and lay it over our ideas of race. Witches do not exist. Race does not exist. But they are real nonetheless. They live in thought and language. I wonder if witches may be more real than races. In my culture, the supernatural is entirely natural. Ancestral spirits are alive.

Racecraft is more evil than witchcraft. That much I do know. The superstition of race has created our nightmares. Racism, like sorcery, confirms the world it assumes already exists. It is the action that creates the evidence. A White man with a gun kills Black people. The TV reporter cannot find it in herself to call him a racist. Not once does she say that. The problem is the colour of Black skin. The problem is always ours.

There is nothing in the hue of a person's skin that creates segregation and suffering; it happens when people act on ideas about that skin colour. Racecraft turns the consequence – imagined colour – into the cause: an individual is discriminated against because they are perceived as Black, not because of the actions of another. The Fields sisters say that although we may have moved beyond fears of witchcraft, racecraft persists. Race, to those who see themselves as White, is entirely rational. The unreasonable division of humankind is itself drawn from the well of White reason.

There were no races before racism made them so. Race is a fiction. But racism is real. It is lethal. It is cruel. It refuses to die. Race is superstition. Racism is criminal intent. As Karen and Barbara Fields write, 'Race belongs to the same family as the evil eye. Racism belongs to the same family as murder and genocide.'

❖

The White Queen is dead.

Karen and Barbara Fields have given me a new language to frame the world. They reject outright the language of race, even terms like 'mixed-race' or 'post-racialism'. They are racist words too. As they write, 'restoring notions of race mixture to centre stage recommits us, willy-nilly, to the discredited idea of racial purity, the basic premise of bio-racism'.

The Fields sisters have set a task that is beyond me. It is beyond Barack Obama. Beyond Meghan Markle. It is beyond my mother, my grandmother, my grandfather. The spell of Whiteness is too strong. It leaves us tongue-tied. Try it. Try it for a day. Try thinking or speaking without any reference to race. I can't. Maybe it is different for those invented White people. It is a conceit of White people to say, after hundreds of years of profiting from Whiteness, that they don't see colour. But I do. I see colour everywhere. I wish I didn't. I wish it were never so. That I did not have to live in a world defined and ranked by colour. But I have seen colour since I can first remember. 'Why are you so Black?' 'N——r.' I have seen colour everywhere, and that colour is White.

Barack Obama was sworn in to the White House. A citadel to White power. A place built by Black slaves. He was not delivering us from race. He was reminding us of racism. The first Black president was hailed as a victory of White progress. *Look how far we have come*, they said. *This is King's dream made real. The land of the free and the home of the brave. God bless America.* In that moment, I was transfixed too. I was spellbound. Hope. Yes, we can. I believed it all. In that moment. I saw Jesse Jackson crying. How could I not cry too?

And then, in the years ahead, there would be more tears. Tears for Trayvon Martin. Tears for Breonna Taylor. Tears for George Floyd. Tears for the lives lost – Black people killed – under the veil of ignorance.

American liberty is a monument to Whiteness. The statue that calls the tired, the poor, the huddled masses yearning to breathe free – the Statue of Liberty – is the statue of a White woman. It is modelled on the Roman godess Libertas. Some say it resembles the French sculptor's mother. Whatever the case, it is a powerful symbol that, in a nation built on genocide and slavery, a White woman calls forth the refuse of teeming shores. A White woman opens her arms to the world. The historian Tyler E. Stovall calls the Statue of Liberty 'the perfect symbol of White freedom'. Why wouldn't it be? Here is a symbol of a nation that itself symbolises modernity. It is the first modern nation, with its promise of freedom masking just how unfree it actually is. France and America are twinned by modernity. The Statue of Liberty binds them, these two nations of Enlightenment revolution, two nations committed to liberty, equality and freedom. But they are two nations whose utopian dreams have also turned to terror.

It was a French scholar of America, Édouard René de Laboulaye, who imagined a grand gift to the United States. He was despondent that France had turned away from the dreams of the French Revolution. Mourning the dashed hopes of the French Republic, Laboulaye looked to the American Dream. Sculptor Frédéric Auguste Bartholdi crafted Laboulaye's dream. In 1886 the statue was inaugurated in New York Harbor. This was a land still haunted by the Civil War. This was meant to be a new land of liberty. But in the decades ahead, the genocidal wars against First Nations people continued. Chinese immigrants were attacked and killed. Chinese labourers were banned from migrating. Puerto Rico was annexed. Hawaii was stolen. Blacks who thought they were free found out that American freedom was truly skin-deep. As Tyler Stovall says, 'by the dawn of the twentieth century it was clear that America would remain a racialized White republic'.

Visiting New York after the White Queen's death, I made the pilgrimage to the Statue of Liberty along with thousands of others. What draws us here? We each come with our own stories, our own memories, and our own ghosts. The statue is many things to many people. It is what we choose it to be. We see it each through our eyes. Yes, the world has made its way to America. It is the embodiment of the promise of renewal. People risk everything to touch the shores of liberty. I feel that here. I am drawn to that flame. What other nation on Earth has made this sacred pact with humanity? But ... there is always but ... What is liberty, really? There is as much hypocrisy here as promise.

Look closely in the information hall; there is a different story. It is the story of those who paid in blood for this America. There is a reminder that when the statue was unveiled not everyone celebrated. The African-American owned *Cleveland Gazette* wrote: 'Shove the Bartholdi Statue, torch and all, into the ocean until the "liberty" of this country ... [exists for the] colored man.' There is a photo of the singer and activist Harry Belafonte, and below his quote: 'Bring it on. Dissent is central to any democracy.' And then there are the words of James Baldwin: 'I would never know what this statue meant to others, she had always been an ugly joke to me.'

Barack Obama came not to bury the racial republic but to praise it. He had to. He had to be the symbol of American redemption. He had to be America's promise. Maybe he believes it. I have seen Black people shed tears and clutch their hearts as they sing the American anthem. Who am I to say they are wrong? I want to believe in America. America is magical to me. That's how it is meant to be. It is Disneyland. America, said Abraham Lincoln, is a dedication to a proposition. What a glorious idea it is. But Obama was not the fulfilment of the proposition. Indeed there is something lost in this moment. Cornel West captures it when he says: this was 'Black spiritual captivity to American idolatry'. It stings to read him but he is right, in that moment of the first Black president, 'Black people become Barack Obama flag wavers rather than Martin King-like cross bearers.'

America is still an idea yet to be realised. Until it is, there are the words of truth from those with an unwavering and unsentimental eye. The words of the slain Malcolm X. The words that speak back to the White Statue of Liberty: 'America has a very serious problem ... America's problem is us. We're her problem. The only reason she has a problem is she doesn't want us here.'

And so a daughter of America, the 'mixed-race' princess, finds out what it is to be a Black woman. She leaves America, returning to the place from whence America came. Meghan Markle finds that there is one truth that binds these two nations, America and Britain, and it is that they are dedicated to a proposition of Whiteness. As I watch her wedding on television, I hear one of the commentators wonder about the future children of Harry and Meghan, children who could be 'all sorts of colours'. She was not talking about Harry's colour.

10

PRECIOUS WHITE LIVES

The White Queen is dead.

A precious White life.

In the days after her death, while Australia mourned, I was called to confront why her life, why these White lives, matter more than mine. What makes them so precious, and hers the most precious of all? This question may be the hardest of all.

The universe plays its tricks at just the right time. Months before, I had agreed to moderate a discussion with the Black South African writer Sisonke Msimang for a festival of dangerous ideas. And for Sisonke and me, what more dangerous idea could there be but Whiteness? Sisonke and I had had many discussions like this. We had appeared on television programs together, and she had interviewed me at book festivals. Although we were from different continents, we were twinned by the idea of race – to Whiteness, we were Black. The title of our event on this day was 'Precious White Lives'.

Although we may speak English, when we are talking to White people we are always involved in an act of translation. Words are heard so differently. It is as though White people are tuned to a different frequency. White people talk about the 'dispossession' of our country. We know it was stolen. White people talk about 'settlement'. We know we were invaded. White people talk about frontier 'conflict'. We know it was genocide. Yes, even when we use English, we are speaking different languages.

Sisonke began her speech on this day in her language, Zulu. After greeting the mostly White audience, she turned to me and said she always feels it helps to speak back to racism when you don't use the racists' tongue. Later, I would thank her in my language, Wiradjuri. But in between we spoke English; we spoke in a language that we hoped those there on this day would understand.

Sisonke came in warrior's clothes. She wore a striking black and white striped dress; her hair and make-up were dazzling; and before she climbed the steps to the stage she tossed off her flat-soled pumps for sharp high heels. She was dressed for business, she said. Impressions matter to us. We will look better, dress sharper, be smarter and speak faster because we have to. Every time we step out in public we are representing our people.

In English, Sisonke told these White people just how precious they are. She quoted from the great pantheon of Black thinkers, those who have blazed our trails. She spoke about 'double consciousness', first coined by the African American philosopher W.E.B. Du Bois, and later popularised again by the Black English writer Paul Gilroy. What is this 'double-consciousness'? For Du Bois, it is the conflict of being both African and American; for Gilroy, to be both European and Black. Sisonke has to ask herself what it means to be Black in Australia and how she feels about what she calls her 'North Star' – South Africa, where for so long to be Black was a crime. For me: is it possible to even call myself an Australian when this nation has tried to erase my family?

Gilroy calls this a relationship of antagonism. It has certainly been that for me. Yes, I have called myself an Australian, yet even then I was never entirely sure what that meant. When I call myself an Australian, it is with no patriotism, but with tenuous allegiance and a heavy heart. Because I know the price of being an Australian. I know that we were never intended to be Australians. When Britain declared us 'British subjects', it was a convenient trick to steal our country and place us under British law. Australia was never designed for us. It was built over us. We were expected to die out.

I was once asked what makes me sad. 'Australia,' I said, and I said it without a moment's hesitation. That's what Australia feels like to me – it feels sad. I have rarely felt more alone than when I have been among other Australians, like the night in 2000 I sat in an enormous stadium for the opening ceremony of the Sydney Olympic Games. There were more than a hundred thousand people there, people I should be able to call my own. They wore smiles, they were excited and proud. Australia was showing its face to the world, and these Australians held their flag aloft. There is nothing in that flag that speaks to me – not the colours or the stars, and not the red and white Union Jack in the corner, the symbol of Britain and a reminder that this land was stolen.

How I wanted to feel what these Australians felt. How I wished I could simply pretend to feel as they felt. Instead I ached for a country that has never been.

As the nations of the world marched into the stadium, I saw the history of the world unfurled. Nations are not real – they are imagined. They are born out of war and invasion and conquest. Nations are bordered, as much to keep people out as in. We think nations are permanent, but they rise and fall.

With each war the borders are redrawn and the people renamed.

Nations speak to empire and they speak to Whiteness. Even those nations that are not 'White' exist because Whiteness has made it so. It was White nations in the seventeenth-century Treaties of Westphalia who established what nations should be. This was how they brought order to slaughter, the treaties ending the Thirty Years' War, which killed more than eight million people. It is White nations who have drawn lines on maps from Africa to the Middle East to Asia and decreed them nations. It was a White nation that erased the hundreds of borders of this ancient land and called it Australia.

I looked around the stadium that night and I saw those flags, all colours and designs. I saw how proudly people marched. I watched Black people who had lived under the boot of colonisers now beaming as they marched for nations they now controlled. I watched North and South Korea, bitter enemies who had massacred each other as only families can do, and who lived divided by an imaginary line that ran like a scar through their land, marching together now, just for this moment. I was proud for them. This is what sport at its best can do. But I felt no pride for myself or for what should be my country. Among all the flags of the world, mine was missing.

That's when you know where you stand. In those moments, we are reminded that we are a people of powerlessness. Our country is gone. It lives in us but where do we find it in law? I can call myself Wiradjuri or Kamilaroi or Dharrawal, and that means something, but to the world we don't exist. That's what the ancestors of the White Queen stole: our right to be who we are in the world. No one in that stadium that night, from any of the nations of the world, mourned our loss. They were consumed by pride. They were here and we were not. Australians looked on and saw the best of themselves. We were there in our own way. Aboriginal dancers were part of the opening ceremony. Our greatest athlete, the runner Cathy Freeman, lit the Olympic flame. Australians congratulated themselves that it was a moment of reconciliation between Black and White, as if Cathy herself could heal two centuries of hurt. But Cathy Freeman lit the flame under an Australian flag.

I was back a few nights later. There, again in a heaving stadium, I saw that same Cathy stand at the starting line for a race to immortality. Even now, two decades later, I can feel the tears brimming in my eyes. I can see her, slight and graceful, powerful and purposeful, clad in that in one-piece hooded suit like a superhero – a Black superhero. Not for a moment did I think she would lose. Cathy always said she could feel her ancestors like the wind under her heels. She ran with a small tattoo on her ankle that read 'cos i'm free'.

There, on that track, she was free. And in her triumph she set me free. On that night, when the world watched our Cathy win a race for the ages, my flag – our flag – a black, red and yellow symbol of who we are, was at centre stage. Cathy ran her victory lap with our flag, and there, in that moment, the sadness disappeared and I felt counted.

There, in that stadium, I confronted my 'double consciousness'. As Du Bois would say, I was 'born with a veil, and gifted with second-sight', which lets me see myself 'through the revelation of another world'. I looked for myself in a world of Australians and could find myself only in a world beyond that Australia. A world broken open by a slight Black girl on a running track.

How Du Bois speaks to people like me and Sisonke Msimang. We know what he meant when he spoke of the 'peculiar sensation' of 'double consciousness'. To look at one's self 'through the eyes of others', and to measure one's soul 'by the tape of a world that looks on in amused contempt and pity'. Du Bois said he always felt his 'two-ness – an American, a Negro; two souls, two thoughts, two unreconciled strivings'.

Paul Gilroy wrote of 'the dislocating, dazzle of "Whiteness"'. This Whiteness orders our world. It certainly defines the terms upon which Black people enter Britain. 'Black history and culture are perceived,' Gilroy says, 'like Black settlers themselves, as an illegitimate intrusion into a vision of authentic British national life.' Black people by their very presence disrupt the idyll of Whiteness. The very notion of what it is to be human is now contested.

That's what Sisonke was doing on this day: disrupting the peace. Shaking the lethargy of the good White people who abhor racism yet are its unquestioned beneficiaries.

There is a price for this courage and intellect, and Sisonke was paying it. The price is paid in pain. For White people to listen, to understand, to feel, Sisonke had to open her veins. She had to bleed for the good White people. For half an hour, Sisonke told these people how their precious lives, their precious White lives, had stripped the skin and soul from people like her, like me, like our parents and grandparents, and how Whiteness still strips the skin and soul from Black people, and how it will keep doing this until it stops – until it cares enough to stop. Sisonke is cursed with 'double consciousness' like me, like Du Bois. Du Bois called it a 'peculiar wrenching of the soul, a peculiar sense of doubt and bewilderment'. We live, he said, a 'double life' with 'double thoughts' that give rise to 'double words'.

We know what we know, and we can't not know it. We know what this Whiteness does to us. And what's worse is that we know that this Whiteness is us too. Here we are with our 'two-ness': Australian and Wiradjuri for me, Australian and Zulu for Sisonke. This is the distance. The distance in the Olympic stadium, the distance that Cathy ran, the distance measured in borders. I looked out on the crowd on this day and I could see the distance, good people staring back at us, listening, but even in English I wondered: *Can they hear?*

11

YINDYAMARRA

The White Queen is dead.

Balladhu Wiradjuri Gibir.

Dyirrimadalinya Badhu Wiradjuri.

Yuin Dhi Wongamar.

Do you understand me? Can you hear me?

Do I need to interpret this language for you? This language that has been here on this land for tens of thousands of years? When I speak the name of my great-great-great-grandfather, Wongamar, do you know who he is? He was here before you came and he is here still in me. But you don't see him. You have brought your voices here. Your languages here. His voice is silenced.

I have lived in and travelled to so many lands, and I have heard the towering babel of languages that speak to who we are on this planet. Words that grow out of the land itself. Words for rivers and mountains and trees. Unique words for things that are universal. Love, hope, laughter, birth, death and pain. In those places I have tried to get my tongue around new sounds. If only to say hello. To say I see them. I hear them. But can you speak to me? Can you hear me?

Let me ask you this: why do you find it so easy to walk through this country as if we are not here?

❃

There is a story that has haunted me since I first read it. It is written by the man the Nobel Prize committee said wrote the Australian continent into world literature. As if the stories of eternity my people spoke, the stories painted on our land didn't matter at all. And they didn't – that's the truth. Not to White people.

This man was White, and he told a story of a land becoming White. I think now how absurdly apt it is that his name was White – Patrick White. And his story was a genesis story of a new White Australia. It begins in a forest. An Eden. It is the story of Stan Parker, who takes his new wife, Amy, into the Australian wilderness to hack out a new life, to build a new people.

> Then the man took an axe and struck the side of a hairy
> tree, more to hear the sound than for any other reason ...
> The silence was immense. It was the first time anything like
> this had happened in that part of the bush.

The first time. The first gunshot. The first foreign words. Swallowed into the silence. The new people with their axes – they can't live in the silence. They need noise. They cling to the places where the trees are cleared. After two centuries, Australians fear the bush. It is where they disappear. The places where people die of thirst and hunger. They write stories of death in these places. Of people who venture too far and never return. They fear evil out there. But the evil is in the noise – the crack of an axe striking a tree – just because it had never before.

Australia is a place where White people vanish. Art and literature and film are obsessed with the people who disappear. A Drysdale barren landscape with a lone figure gazing into the distance. A train that stops in a dusty town, and a night of dystopian terror. Booze and vomit and piss, and always the haze of violence. Kangaroos in the headlights and blood smeared on glass. An endless lap of the main street. Just a deadening, stultifying emptiness. It always seems to me that silence scares Australians. In these places there is death. Children snatched from the beach and never again seen. Girls in white dresses on a picnic on Valentine's Day who never return.

So Australians cling to what they know. They lose themselves in crowds. Drown out their thoughts in noise. The hum of traffic lulls them to sleep. If there is a building on the horizon, then they are safe. Australians don't live in the wide brown land. They cling to the coast and the big cities. They don't trust the place even when they tell themselves they have conquered it.

There are many things I do not understand about White people. I see them at the beach near my home. I watch as they dress their children in the same uniforms and caps and march them up and down the sand. They put in flags and mark space with rope. They blow whistles. Children run and jostle past each other. They swarm into the water, kicking, with flailing arms. They turn this water into a battleground. Everything is a competition. Someone must win and someone must lose. Everything – even the beach – must be conquered. The thing is, among all this noise and order I so rarely hear laughter.

I see people at the beach claim their territory. They bring

tents that are sometimes bigger than the houses or caravans I lived in as a child. They hammer in pegs and tie it all down with rope. Just as they have flattened and fenced the whole country. This is theirs now. No one may enter. It feels to me like another invasion. They are possessing the beach. It is not enough that there is sand and water and sun. It is not enough that they can shade themselves with a towel or a hat or a small umbrella. They must own it.

I like to walk early in the morning along the beach and onto the rocks to feel the wind and the sun. To look out at water that people have looked out at forever. To sense the timeless land. I want to walk softly, with no one knowing I am there. All around me, even at dawn, there are people walking heavy. Striding with purpose. I see them walking three or four abreast. They take up room. Rarely do they move aside. As I walk towards them, they continue straight ahead. This they claim as their right. This is their place. I move to one side and let them pass.

What is this need to possess? I ask myself this over and over. Even a walk along the beach becomes an act of ownership. This is what happens when people have been at the centre of all they survey. This is what it means to colonise. It isn't to claim a country. It is to work it. Tilling the soil. Turning it over. The land is tamed for profit. Untold wealth has been extracted from our country. A quarter-acre in the right place in the right city can be a gold mine. A source of limitless wealth.

Great riches cover up our crimes. And we Australians are among the richest people to have ever walked the Earth. Who has to face the past when we go the beach, kick a ball, light a barbecue? There are days I fall in love with Australia. I am seduced by it all. When I sit under a blue sky, I watch the people walk by, people of all colours and cultures. I see veiled Muslim women, their arms and legs fully covered, sitting alongside bikinied girls and shirtless men. I see Black and White couples holding hands and walking with their children. *This is a miracle*, I tell myself. No one here holds the hatred of history. Not today, at least, not while the sun is shining. I catch a glimpse of what we can be. And then I ask myself: *Am I wrong?*

Can I put aside all these questions about race, about the past? Those questions seem ridiculous right at that moment, surrounded by visions of peace and beauty. Does the Brown-skinned girl clasping the hands of her Black father and White mother need to choose between her parents? Can't she block out all the noise and hate, all the racism and let it all go? Maybe she can. Maybe she can believe in this mirage. Maybe we can all believe in it, because the stakes are so low here. There is so little to fight for or about. This Australia is sedated. This Australia is a refuge from history. The people who have come here have often escaped tyranny or war or economic collapse. They don't want home to follow them, and here it doesn't have to. They can cast it all aside and buy into the great forgetting – that is the deal. Under the sun, in the sand, with the taste of salt on their skin, they can do that. This is what it means to become an Australian.

And that's where I wake from the beautiful dream. Because there is no escape for me. My history is here. I don't follow it; it follows me. These people in all their colours and cultures and glory can sing about Australia in ways I cannot. I am, you are, we are Australian; no, not yet. They sing about an Australia I cannot know. And it breaks my heart that this cannot be mine.

And this is what separates me from this dream. Australia is many good things, but the good things all come after the great sin. Nothing can right the wrongs of this nation. There is the possibility of atonement but Australia has not earned that. So I watch the dream and I know it cannot be mine, because all of this was stolen from us.

❋

The White Queen is dead.

I entered the world of White Australia as an invisible man. In the words of Ralph Ellison, 'people refuse to see me'. People like me wonder if we are not phantoms ourselves – ghosts. As Ellison put it, we want to be real, we ache with the need to convince ourselves that we exist. But we are just figments of the imagination: in Ellison's case, of the White imagination. We appear only in the inner eyes of those who look upon us. I have lived this transformation – from a Black boy among other Black boys, to the only Black boy in a White school, to a Black boy on White television – and with each incarnation I became more visible, more 'real', until now I am deemed worthy of the great White compliment: 'But you're not like the others ...'

So Ellison says we have a choice: to strike out violently, hurting those who cannot see us until they cannot deny us, or to embrace our invisibility and 'walk softly so as not to awaken the sleeping ones'. As Ellison wrote, 'it is possible to carry on a fight against them without their realising it'. The invisible man is a man without history. He is not born, he is discovered. And the invisible man spends forever trying to be seen. To make White people see what they want to see.

When I was fifteen, we moved from my hometown, Griffith, to Canberra. The pattern of our lives continued. A new job for Dad. A new place to call home for us. But this was the most foreign place I had ever been. The Whitest place on Earth – or so it seemed then. I had always lived among other

Aboriginal people – my family, cousins, and friends – now my sister and I were the only Black kids in the school. I didn't understand anything around me: not the people I met, the clothes they wore, the way they spoke. Nothing.

I had never spent much time in a White person's house. I had lived alongside White people – Whites who were dirt poor like us – but never White people like this. These kids whose fathers came home from work clean, and who had lived in the same houses all their lives and had the same friends from childhood. The smart-arse racist remarks started on day one, so I had a choice: I could fight my way from one day to the next, or I could shut up and get along. I swallowed my pride, laughed at their jokes and shrank a little bit inside. I learned what every Aboriginal person – every Black or non-White person – learns: we don't make the rules and we don't have the power.

Historian Bob Reece says Aborigines 'were both an invention and product of European colonisation'. There were no 'Aborigines' here until White people arrived and named us. Hundreds of different peoples or tribes – or nations, as we now call them – were produced in the White imagination as a homogenous group. Aborigines become part of a national narrative: the noble savage fading from the frontier; the doomed race. Always fixed in someone else's imagination.

In this world I had to find a way to break free. Like Ellison's invisible man, I have wanted to be seen as a human being. Ellison's narrator needs to find a place beyond belonging, beyond even Blackness. A place of freedom. But race is always there. He is forced underground to wrestle with the demons of race and violence. In telling the story we might be free. That is all we have. In my life I have searched for the beautiful soul inside me. According to Gilles Deleuze, the beautiful soul says: 'we are different but not opposed'.

The beautiful soul threads the needle of the twin tensions of modernity: tradition and progress. We need tradition to ground us. We are rootless otherwise. Yet progress pushes us onward. Without it, we can't think new thoughts. Between tradition and progress is the restless beautiful soul. Tradition holds us back and progress leaves us untethered. Modernity arrives at a fork in the road: one way lies freedom, the other way certainty. The devil waits for us down both roads. That is modernity's blessing and its curse.

❉

The White Queen is dead.

Sisonke and I wear a single garment of destiny. It was the same Crown that claimed her land for the British Empire that invaded and colonised mine. The same White Queen – then a princess – spoke to her subjects on her twenty-first birthday from the land of Sisonke's people. It was 1947, one year before apartheid officially began. Apartheid means 'apartness' in Afrikaans. What it truly meant was White superiority. It meant terror. It meant that people who were not White were deemed not truly human – not in the way White people were human. Apartheid has become a term synonymous with evil.

When the White Princess spoke, apartheid was not official policy, but it existed nonetheless. The term was first used as far back as 1917. Apartheid was not an invention of the Afrikaners but a legacy of empire. It was British colonialism that introduced laws separating people by race. In the nineteenth century, Britain imposed laws regulating the movement of Black people. Blacks were not allowed onto the streets in towns in the Cape Colony after dark. They had to carry a special pass with them. Blacks and non-White people across the country were banned from voting, with only a few select exceptions.

When the White Princess spoke from South Africa, she said she was speaking to all peoples of the Commonwealth and Empire, whatever race they came from. But she mentioned nothing of equality or justice for all. She did not speak against a racial hierarchy that stripped the skin from people's backs and stole the land from under their feet. She spoke of hardship and anxiety. She spoke of the war just two years ended. She told of the great defence of liberty, and of how, in her words, 'God has matched us with this hour'. But where was the liberty for Black people?

She spoke of how the British Empire had 'saved the world'. She declared that her whole life, whether it be long or short, would be devoted to the service of the great imperial family. But who belonged to that imperial family? Were they Black people in South Africa, who were denied full citizenship in their own land? Were my people her people? In 1947, we were not even counted among the population of Australia. Laws restricted our movement. Aboriginal people had to apply for exemptions – dog collars, we called them – to enjoy the freedoms that White people took as their God-given right. My grandfather had fought in a war for the British Empire, but returned home to a nation that would not allow him to share a drink in a pub with the men he fought alongside. The White Princess was not speaking to him. When the White Princess spoke, she was talking to White people. She was certainly not speaking to non-White people – not there in South Africa or here in Australia.

The White Princess spoke to her subjects from a land where Britain had perfected modern war and rehearsed cruelty that would inspire the great sin of the twentieth century. In South

Africa, White Britons waged war on Black Africans and White Afrikaners. The British had taken control of the Cape Colony from the Dutch in 1806, and sought to bring both the Black and the White populations of the neighbouring Boer republics under their control. The Boer War broke out in 1899. Britain proclaimed it a war against the racist Boer state, but really it was a war over wealth: gold and land. It was a war in which Whiteness was the only imagined winner.

The British high commissioner in Cape Town, Alfred Milner, said that 'the ultimate end is a self-governing White community supported by well treated and justly governed Black labour'. 'Well treated' and 'justly governed', but Black people would never control their own destiny. Milner described himself as 'an imperialist' and a 'British race patriot'. Black people were expendable: 'You have only to sacrifice the "nigger" absolutely,' he said. A budding young race patriot named Winston Churchill was dispatched to cover the war as a reporter.

In South Africa, the British modelled warfare to come. At the helm was Horatio Herbert (later Lord) Kitchener, the man whose face, with its flamboyant moustache, would stare down from recruitment posters to demand the ultimate sacrifice from a generation of Britons in the First World War. Kitchener 'racialised' the White Afrikaners exactly as the British had applied race politics to the Irish. The Afrikaners were 'primitive', and were described as an 'infestation'. Whiteness is never about White skin. It is about power. It is about imposing a hierarchy of civilisation, with Whiteness – the idea – at the top.

In South Africa, Kitchener honed a cruel, dehumanising strategy that was first trialled in India. Thousands of 'rebellious' Indians were herded into labour camps. These people were described as a virus, 'infecting' the population. In the camps these people would be starved into submission. Kitchener perfected these cruel camps in South Africa. The historian Caroline Elkins describes them as 'concentration camps … punitive hostage sites'. Not only were Afrikaner guerrillas rounded up. Women and children too became 'legitimate targets for violence'. Like the Indians before them, these people were described as 'verminous'. Their rations were reduced to 'weaken them'. As Elkins says, 'the establishment of the British concentration camps in South Africa were the first time a single ethnic group had been targeted en masse'. We know, of course, where this innovation would lead in the decades to come: the death camps of Nazi Germany.

In Britain there was outrage. Politicians and activists like welfare campaigner Emily Hobhouse railed against the brutal tactics the British used against the Afrikaners. Hobhouse was derided as hysterical. Later, when she tried to visit South

Africa, Kitchener had her forcibly detained and deported. But others, including a future prime minister, David Lloyd George, criticised Britain's concentration camps, calling it a 'policy of extermination'. While there was outrage at the treatment of White Afrikaners, where were the voices protesting the abuse of Black people?

Kitchener sent tens of thousands of Blacks – some of whom even supported the British war on the Boers – to the concentration camps. As Elkins describes it, these camps 'were worse than those of the Afrikaners. Emaciated and disease ridden, Blacks undertook forced labour for reduced rations, and their death rates climbed, conservatively, to over 10 percent of the camp populations.'

Ultimately, Black people were the most victimised of all. With the negotiated treaty to end the Boer War, Whites kept their self-government within the British Empire. They were given millions of pounds to reconstruct their country. Blacks were condemned to a century of White rule. In a war where White fought White, Whiteness was the winner.

In 1947, when the young White Princess spoke to her empire, the world was on tilt. Two years after the end of the Second World War, a new order was taking shape. We call it a 'global rules-based order', but really it was a power-based order. A race-based order. The triumphant White nations were shaping the contours of our lives. Our economies, our borders, our rights. Ahead lay years of war and uprisings. The dead would number in the millions. The colonial world was being upended as Whiteness itself was digging in.

The Bretton Woods agreement had been signed just a few years earlier, establishing the International Monetary Fund and the World Bank, both dominated by Europeans and Americans. The US dollar was fixed as the international currency weighted against gold. The state of Israel was created in 1948. The United Nations carved out territory from British-held Palestine. War soon followed, and conflict has never truly ceased there. India threw off British colonial rule, gaining independence. India and Pakistan drew a line between themselves. Tens of millions were displaced, and millions are estimated to have died in the violence. The two nations today remain locked in an existential, nuclear-armed stand-off. In 1949, China's Communist Party claimed victory in a civil war that set the nation on a new path.

In Kenya, the Mau Mau rebellion would soon break open. Between 1952 and 1960, fighting between the Kenya Land and Freedom Army and the British killed thousands. A thousand Kenyans were executed. And that's only the official number; the Kenya Human Rights Commission says ninety thousand Mau Mau and other rebels were executed. More than a hundred thousand were imprisoned in camps that have been called British gulags. People were tortured, beaten and starved. All this slaughter happened with the White Queen on the throne.

In 1947, five years before her coronation, this was the world, present and emerging, that the White Princess could have spoken of in her birthday address. She could have spoken of violence and concentration camps and racism. But she spoke of empire and civilisation and saving the world. We could say this was just the times. The White Princess was just a young woman. We could make all manner of excuses. But she of all people knew what was right and what was wrong. She had lived through a war against the most heinous threat to humanity, Hitler's Nazi Germany. She had seen millions of Jews sent to Nazi concentration camps. Her nation had sacrificed its young in this fight. Ideas of freedom and equality had been alive in the world for centuries. She knew what evil was, yet she could not speak its name when she saw it before her own eyes.

This is what Whiteness does: it blinds us. It stops us from seeing Black suffering as we do White suffering. Black people were people to be saved, rescued from barbarism, and brought in to 'civilisation'. To the White Princess, we were invisible.

※

What South Africa teaches us is that White people – those who believe themselves White – will decide what Whiteness is. They will determine who gets to be White. They will define Whiteness and define it again. The British decided that the Irish were not White; they were vermin. The British decided that the Afrikaners, in that time of war, were not White. Like the Irish, the Afrikaners were an infestation. Whiteness – I say it again and again and again – is not about skin colour. There is no Blackness, there is no 'other', until those who claim Whiteness for themselves decide what Blackness is, and what the 'other' is. Whiteness is always the province of power. Whiteness is invented, then it is inflicted.

The Irish got to become White. Just as the Afrikaners perfected Whiteness. When the Irish came to my country, they found a new people to be Black. The Irish were as brutal here as the British were to them. I know. I carry the name of an Irishman driven from his country. Here he became landed gentry. He took what was ours. He bred Black children and cast us aside. That part of me that is Irish I have never been able to claim. Here, I am Black.

I wonder: in all the world, are we not the Blackest of all? If Whiteness looks on Blackness and sees something less than human, is that us? Toni Morrison said Ralph Ellison was wrong – Black people were not invisible … not to each other.

But we were invisible to Whiteness. And so many White people in Australia fail to see us still. If this is how Whiteness defines Blackness, as something despised, are we the 'Blackest' of all?

Africans taken to America in chains have seen a Black man in the White House. They are a voice that will not be silenced. Native Americans, those called Indians, who were slaughtered and driven from their lands, have treaties. Not always honoured, that is true, but I have been to Indian land and I know when I am there that I am on Indian land. Sovereign land. In India, they had Gandhi. They have independence. South Africa had Mandela. In New Zealand, Māori people have the Treaty of Waitangi, and their language is spoken. Pakeha – White New Zealanders – know whose lands they are on.

But what of us? No treaties. No recognition. No self-determination. We are as Noel Pearson – the Aboriginal lawyer and community leader – said in his 2022 Boyer Lecture: the 'unloved'. Marcia Langton, a fierce advocate for our people, someone who has influenced the direction of my life more than any other outside my family, has said that to call this racism is not enough. It is more than that. We have been despised. When the British looked upon us, they saw something not fully human.

The British knew what human was. They knew what was right and what was wrong. In England in the 1770s, before the invasion of this land, abolitionists were campaigning to end slavery. The Quakers had long preached that slavery was un-Christian. Some Enlightenment philosophers saw it as a violation of 'the rights of man'. By the mid-1780s, William Wilberforce – ultimately the leader of the movement to abolish the slave trade – had formed the Clapham Sect, a group of social reformers seeking to liberate slaves. The British abolitionists influenced movements in the United States and Canada. By the 1790s, an act had been passed to limit slavery in parts of Canada. While the British Empire was still conquering other lands, no one could pretend they were not too conquering people – human beings.

The First Fleet dropped anchor here when the world was ablaze with debate and ideas about what it was to be human. The Declaration of Independence had been written in the United States, asserting that 'all men are created equal', even as America's founding fathers held slaves themselves. In 1789 the French Revolution exploded, beginning the world anew. What we know as modernity was taking shape. But we were considered primitive. Not long for this world. By the time Australia became a nation, they were smoothing our dying pillow.

✻

Sisonke lives in my country, and when her South Africa was finally throwing off the yoke of apartheid I was there. I travelled to South Africa to watch a nation change. In 1990 Nelson Mandela was finally released from prison. The one-time revolutionary leader of the armed wing of the African National Congress, a man who met White force with Black resistance, would in a couple of years become South Africa's first Black president. But at that moment, while the walls between White and Black were being torn down, old habits and old hatreds were dying hard.

I reported from across South Africa, venturing into a world beyond the cities where White people were trying to hold back the tide. I travelled into one tiny town, Orania, a White enclave in a nation of Black people. Here the Whites had expelled everyone of dark skin. For me it was like walking onto a movie set, or some carefully scripted grotesque reality show where White people were actors in their own utopia. It was a town that time had forgotten. And that's how they wished it to be. Right there, right then, I was the darkest person to walk those streets.

I met a woman there. She was a mother and a wife who, I am sure, loved in her own way. She affected a kindness and a cool grace. Her face was fixed in a permanent smile, but her eyes showed no warmth at all. They were dead. She told me how the Blacks were different – not that she had anything against them, she insisted, but they came from another world to hers. Everything about her was measured, and she was careful to betray no hatred. But what else could this be? This was a town that would not accept me, let alone a Black or so-called 'coloured' South African.

Orania, I thought back then, might be the last White town on Earth. If there was another place like it, I had neither seen it nor heard of it. In that tiny speck on the map, Whiteness was making its last stand. Everywhere on Earth we have been thrown together: people of all colours and faiths and cultures and languages. We cannot avoid each other, even if we still cannot accept each other. But Orania was evil. Although its people called themselves Christians, I could feel the malevolence as I walked the streets of that town. Time there was frozen; its people existed as if in some twilight world.

I asked the woman with the forced smile what she would do if her daughter married a Black man. I wanted to get past the veneer. I needed to find this woman's pulse. She could speak to me so dispassionately about racial differences and culture and freedom, but what are those things if they do not become blood and flesh? I knew that every minute I spent in her presence was an effort for her. I knew that I disgusted her. Now I was asking about her flesh, her blood, her daughter.

She did not answer at first, but the smile vanished. What would she do? I pressed again. If her daughter married a Black man, she said, then she would have no place in Orania. Her daughter would sleep in her bed as she made it, the woman said.

Orania is still there, years later. Still the last White town on Earth. Its numbers have grown. It prints its own currency. Only Afrikaans is spoken, and the residents fear an outside world that would weaken their Afrikaner culture. They have a word, *selfwerksaamheid*, which means self-reliance. Everything they do for themselves. It is not enough to call them White. To these people, Whiteness itself has lost its meaning, its purpose. The ancestors of these people first came to the Cape of Good Hope in the seventeenth century. Their blood is in the soil. To the people of Orania, Whiteness has surrendered. Ask them if they are White and they will likely say no. They are Afrikaners. The Whitest of all.

When Sisonke sits down, I want to say thank you, but thank you is too easy. Thank her for what? For surviving that awful, inhumane apartheid regime? For telling us what should be apparent: that we people who are deemed not human are human too? How can I thank her for suffering again and again and again? Thank you isn't enough. Sorry, I say.

I am sorry, Sisonke, that you have to plead for peace and love and respect, I tell her. I am sorry that in this week, when the precious White life of the White Queen is so mourned, you have to speak of lives that are so unloved and unmourned – of your life – of our lives – and of the lives of those we love.

Thank you is easy. Thank you spoken in English is too easy.

Yindyamarra. Respect.

Mandang Guwu. That's better. Not English but my Wiradjuri. Mandang Guwu, from me to you, with no translation. Thank you.

12

UNFORGIVABLE BLACKNESS

The White Queen is dead.

And Sisonke Msimang has told us of a King. A Black King. A Black King who walked across the world with his head unbowed. A Black King – the first Black King – who conquered the White world. He stood over Whiteness with his hands held aloft. A fist in the air and a smile on his face. We had never before seen one such as this. This Black King hit like a thunderbolt, he swayed and danced, took a hit and grinned right back. This Black King was transgressive. This Black King took what Whiteness held as its right, he battered the White world and reduced it to hope.

The Black King's name was Jack Johnson, heavyweight champion of the world. The first Black King of the ring. They would all follow: Muhammad Ali, Joe Frazier, George Foreman, Mike Tyson, Lennox Lewis. But the Black King was the first.

Jack Johnson had unforgivable Blackness.

In 1908 Jack Johnson claimed his title here in Australia. It had been a long road. For years he had been considered the greatest fighter in the world. He had terrorised opponents everywhere. But he could never get a title shot. No White champion would fight him. Jim Jeffries retired rather than face Johnson. Finally Jack Johnson got his chance against Tommy Burns. Burns was the great White hope. He was the reigning heavyweight champion of the world. This would be more than a title fight. When Jack Johnson touched gloves with Tommy Burns, he was touching off a race war. That's exactly what the Australian media called it: a race war.

Racism has never been far from sport in Australia. It probably starts here with this title fight. Jack Johnson was a Black man Australia had never seen. There had been Black warriors here, those who fought the British invaders. In the early years of the colony, they threatened at times to drive the coloniser back into the sea. But Australia was a fact now. Just a few years earlier, the states had come together to form a federation. This was a White nation dedicated to keeping the 'coloured races' out. And here was Jack Johnson dressed like a dandy, with White women hanging off his arm, a hat tilted to the side and a taunting smile.

Johnson loved to beat up White people. When he fought Black men he prevailed too, but those bouts were more playful – exhibitions really – as Johnson carried his brothers through the rounds confident they could not touch him. Against White fighters, it was said, he vented all of his anger, his humiliation. And he humiliated them.

Tommy Burns had talked a good fight. He'd said he would beat Johnson or his name wasn't Tommy Burns. Funny, that – it wasn't. His real name was Noah Brusso. And Noah Brusso and Tommy Burns together could not beat Jack Johnson. Johnson had pursued Burns all around the world. Mocking him. Challenging him. Finally, money spoke. Burns would pocket thirty thousand dollars, twice what any previous fighter had been paid.

Sydney built a new stadium for the event. Look at photos of the fight – a crush of White men. In the ring is the physically beautiful Jack Johnson – tall, sinewy, muscles rippling. The diminutive Tommy Burns almost disappears in the shadow of the giant Johnson. The photos reveal the mismatch that the fight was. But White people never believe their eyes. They are blinded by dazzling Whiteness. It was obvious what would happen in this fight, but it was also unthinkable. Jack London, the sportswriter and famous novelist, had travelled from the United States to cover the 'race war' and he set the tone. London said he was 'with Burns all the way. He is a White man and so am I.'

There were twenty thousand White men in that outdoor arena to cheer on Burns. What they saw was a demolition. Johnson dropped Burns in the first round. It could have been over just as it had begun. But Johnson had not come this far merely to win a fight. He knew he would walk away with the title. He knew he had one hand on history. Johnson was here to tell the world that Black lives mattered, a century before that slogan would echo around the world. Johnson would not let Burns fall. Reporters ringside tell of Johnson propping up the smaller man, hitting him with carefully placed body shots. Moving in and then moving out. Johnson hit Burns, then let him recover, then hit him again. All Burns had to throw were racial insults. And with every taunt, Johnson hit him again. Finally the referee ended it. Jack London had to concede this was not a fight but a massacre, 'the playful Ethiopian at loggerheads with a small and futile White man'.

Back home in the United States, Black people were being lynched. In one year there were nearly seventy lynchings – Black people strung up and murdered by White vigilantes. When the news broke that Jack Johnson had taken a White man's crown,

Black people rejoiced. They turned out in their tens of thousands to celebrate in towns and cities all across America. White mobs attacked them. Violent riots broke out everywhere. Estimates of the dead top two dozen. In Houston, Texas, a man named Charles Williams had his throat slashed by a White man while riding on a streetcar. In New York, thousands of White people ransacked Black neighbourhoods, setting fire to buildings and assaulting Black people. One report said a 'negro was clubbed to death and more than 100 people beaten up'. Another Black man was 'seized by angry Whites and strung up on a lamppost. He was nearly dead when the police cut him down.' Black people retaliated by stabbing or shooting White people.

When he returned to America, Jack London began the search for a White hero to rise and take back what the Black man had claimed. London wrote that 'the White man must be rescued'. He invented the myth of the great White hope – the White man who would avenge Burns' defeat. All eyes turned to the retired former champion Jim Jeffries, a giant of a man who had refused to meet a Black man in the ring.

When Jeffries climbed into the ring with Johnson, it was hailed as the fight of the century. Like the fight with Burns, this was another race war. *The New York Times*, the newspaper of record, wrote that if the Black man wins, 'thousands of his ignorant brothers will misinterpret his victory as justifying claims to much more than mere physical equality with their White neighbours'. Jeffries, like Tommy Burns, never stood a chance. Johnson destroyed him.

Jack Johnson, the first Black King, scandalised the White world. He had a White girlfriend, Lucille Cameron, who would later become his wife. In 1912, Johnson was arrested and convicted of taking Cameron across state lines. This was illegal under a racial purity law that forbade relationships between Black and White. Johnson was charged under what was known as the *Mann Act* but was in fact titled the *White-Slave Traffic Act*. Johnson fled to Europe, where he made his living fighting exhibition matches. But he returned to America and was jailed for nearly a year. He died in a car crash in 1946.

His shadow still looms over sport – and there have been many Jack Johnsons since. Black athletes with their fists held high, Black athletes who take a knee, and Black athletes who pay a price for being Black.

❖

The White Queen is dead.

In the same week, an Australian Rules footballer, a Black man, Eddie Betts, says that in this country he feels far too often like he does not belong.

I am watching Eddie Betts on television, on a panel surrounded by White people. I can see his shoulders tense, I can see him biting down hard on his jaw. His breath looks like it is caught somewhere in his chest – even through the screen I can see he is suffocating. Eddie looks down and then off to the side. He knows what he wants to say but I know he is wondering whether he should say it. He is wondering how he should say it. That's what we do – we learn to check ourselves. To measure our words. Speaking truth is not enough; we have to ask: *What will people do with that truth?* We know – Eddie Betts surely knows – the price we can pay for speaking that truth.

Eddie is telling the White men on the television show what his life is like as a Black man in their Australia. He tells them about being followed by security guards when he goes shopping. He tells them about being at a swimming pool with his children, and how a White lifeguard asked them to get out. An elderly White couple, he says, complained that Eddie Betts and his children were making their grandchild uncomfortable. This is what we live with, he says, every day. This is what we live with. This is why he doesn't feel like he belongs, here in Australia. This is what Aboriginal people experience, he says. Only his wife keeps him here. She tells him that he, above anyone, should feel like he belongs, because this is his country.

Eddie Betts carries what could be an unbearable burden. But he bears it. He carries that load because he knows he does not play just for himself. He does not speak just for himself. He is not just an athlete – like Jack Johnson, he is more than an athlete. He is a symbol. His presence alone is a lightning rod for all of Australia's unresolved, messy, hateful, hurtful legacy of race. People read into him all of their history. To other Indigenous people – to me – he sounds like home. To White people, I know he can sound like a problem, something to be fixed; something to be pitied, perhaps, or even admired. To those most bitter and twisted, he is something to be reviled. But he can never slip the knot of race. He can never simply be an athlete.

The White Queen is dead and Eddie Betts is being asked to explain again what Whiteness does. This is what we ask of him.

A few months earlier, I was with Eddie and our great champion Cathy Freeman. We were speaking about race to White university students. I ask Cathy again about that night in Sydney in that Olympic Stadium in 2000 and the race that set her free. I tell her again – I tell her every time I see her – what that night meant to me. I ask her to relive it again, to take me through that race. What was she thinking? Was she aware of the crowd? The other runners? When she crossed the finish line and sat there blinking, was she lost? Where did she go? So, so, so many questions, and she can't possibly answer them all. But her answer surprises me.

I don't go there, she says. She tells me that she has never really processed it. Why would she? How could she? I realise then that it would be like trying to answer Australia.

This is what the White men on the television were really asking Eddie to do. They wanted him to explain Australia. Eddie is being asked to bare his soul, to reveal his torment, so that they might understand. And somewhere out there people are spreading their poison. They will attack him where he hurts the most, and by then the White men asking these questions will be back in the safety of their Australia and Eddie will be shielding his family, his children, the children he held in that swimming pool, those children who so offended the old White couple – he will be defending them from that same Australia that makes him feel like he doesn't belong.

Why was Eddie here? Because in this week when the White Queen died, Australian football was mired again in racism. The sport Eddie Betts played was front-page news, and for the same old reasons. Time and again it ends up here with Aboriginal people or Black people defending themselves against a sport – and a country – that tells them they don't belong. This time it was the Hawthorn club. It could just as easily have been any of a dozen clubs. The game was shocked. Again. People were outraged. Again. Again we heard the same comments. The game must do better. We should all learn. There must be an inquiry. The same comments, just like the time before, and the time before that, and the time before that. Everyone was shocked but us.

The truth in this case, we were told, would in time be revealed. But we already knew the ugly truths of the Australian Football League. This is the game where a senior club official once said Aboriginal people would be admired and respected if they 'conduct themselves like White people'. If they 'conduct themselves like human beings'. This is the game where a club official once said that only Aboriginal players with at least one parent should be recruited. This is the game where crowds viciously abused the Aboriginal player Nicky Winmar. Nicky was one of the most talented players in the game, and he always attracted attention. He was used to being heckled and abused. Then on one day in a game against Collingwood in 1993, the racism went to a new and frightening level. He has said that people in the crowd made violent threats, taunting him and other Black players. Some in the crowd made the vilest comments about his mother and sisters. Nicky responded as he knew how, by playing better. And then, in triumph, he stared them down and he lifted his football jersey revealing his Black skin and he pointed to it as if to say, *This is who I am.*

This is the game that allowed Adam Goodes to be relentlessly booed into retirement. Goodes was perhaps the most gifted player of his generation. Twice he won the award as the game's best. He was more than a footballer. Adam became a voice; he spoke back when others fell silent. He saw racism and he called it out. There was a lifetime of tears in Adam Goodes' success. His mother's tears. A Black woman taken from her family – stolen – cut adrift from her culture. She lost her language. She lost her land. These things are never put right. But she held her boys close and she carried them from town to town and she raised a man who would make sure his mother's story did not go untold.

Adam Goodes was named Australian of the Year in 2014. He dedicated the award to fighting racism. He spoke of bringing Black and White together. As he was a champion on the field, so he would be a champion of reconciliation. The year before, Adam Goodes had been called an 'ape' by a young girl in the crowd. Hearing the slur but not knowing who had made it, Goodes turned around and furiously pointed, demanding the person be removed. The incident exploded. It was headline news. Everyone had had a view and some commentators blamed Goodes himself, even though Adam called for people not to blame the girl, and himself reached out to her. He was accused of victimising her. Adam became the thing White people fear, the angry Black man.

This moment would define Adam Goodes' career. He had overcome so many things. He could not overcome this. By 2015 he was a broken figure. He had been booed over and over, game after game after game. Each time he would touch the ball he would be met with a torrent of boos. Inside stadiums, the booing resounded with such force that at times it sounded like a jet plane taking off. Off the field, Adam Goodes was taunted and told to 'toughen up'. This man who had never sought favours and never ducked a challenge was accused of playing the 'victim'. That's what we are called when we speak truth. When we tell of how this nation's history shapes our souls, is absorbed into our DNA, we are told that we are being victims.

Adam Goodes went home. Where we go when we need to draw strength. He sat under trees. He listened to stories. He felt the earth. He returned to the field and then he walked away. He has never been back.

✻

The White Queen is dead.

News is breaking that the Hawthorn Football Club has been accused of traumatising First Nations players and their families, bullying them, removing them from their homes, separating them from loved ones, asking them to make a choice: their careers or their families. All of this emerged out of a club review. The allegations ranged from the troubling to the disgusting. Two players said they were pressured into removing SIM cards from their phones so their partners could not contact them. But in the worst case, the club allegedly attempted to intimidate one couple into terminating a pregnancy.

For Black people in this week, this is what Australia looks like. White Australia is in mourning and Black people are mourning too. But as is so often the case, two peoples are mourning two very different versions of the same country. What timing. At moments like this, histories collide. The Crown is the very symbol of invasion and conquest; the crimes committed under that Crown amount to crimes against humanity itself. And we, the First Peoples of this land, have lived in a shadow world. Our history has been hidden. The Hawthorn allegations reinforce that history. Australia has invaded the bodies of Black people. We have been shot, poisoned, our heads have been severed and sent back to England as trophies. We have had chains around our necks. Black women have been violated. We have been measured and divided, defined and redefined more than sixty times as British law decided what type of human we were. Now here is a story of bodies invaded, families separated, and all of it in a game that had made Black players feel like they do not belong.

We could call this racism. But racism is not a strong enough word. It falls too easily from people's lips. It is usually followed by a promise to do better. To call inquiries. To listen and learn. To collaborate. Often Black people are brought in to help, to work so that White people might be better. But we know that the perpetrators of racism too often pay no price. There are people in senior positions, working on television, commentating games, who have been guilty of racism. Racism bears little shame in Australia. For White people there is always a way back.

Let's swap the word racism for violence – because that's what it is – and then ask if racists should keep their jobs. Violence was committed against Nicky Winmar, against Adam Goodes, against Eddie Betts and so many other people of colour. These latest allegations against officials at Hawthorn are violent in their depravity. Racism kills. Who is held to account for this violence? Sport, we are told, is a place beyond politics. A place beyond race. A place where talent is all that matters. That is a myth. Sport should build allegiance but it often reveals – indeed, widens – societies' racial fault lines.

We might like to believe that we are a different nation than we were a century ago. We might like to think we have moved on from the time twenty thousand White men crammed into an outdoor stadium to bray for a Black man's blood. How comforting it is to think that the race war between Tommy Burns and Jack Johnson belongs to another time. But that would be a lie. Yes, there have been examples of well-loved Indigenous sports heroes: Lionel Rose, Evonne Goolagong, Cathy Freeman, more recently Ash Barty. But there has always been an expectation that they will be modest and respectful and stay out of politics. Outspoken Indigenous athletes, like former rugby league star and world champion boxer Anthony Mundine, weren't so loved. Many people paid their money hoping he would be defeated.

Indigenous footballers who represent our national teams will not sing our national anthem. This country rings hollow to them. Australia, for far too many, is a nation without honour. The same can be said of our national game. The AFL cannot just pledge to do better next time. There have been too many apologies. Too many broken hearts. Too many broken lives. One thing we know, sadly, is that the Hawthorn investigation will not be the last. The game cannot rid of itself of racism, because the AFL mirrors our society.

No wonder it is called Australian Rules.

❋

The White Queen is dead.

And if only this is the last of it. But in the weeks after the White Queen's death, another Black athlete is in the middle of a firestorm. Donnell Wallam is a netball player, and only the third First Nations player in the history of the sport to be selected for Australia. That fact alone should demand condemnation. How can a sport so ignore an entire section of our society? Not just any section, but the First People of the land? Wallam had to leave Australia and live and play in England to be noticed in her own country. But, like Adam Goodes and Eddie Betts and Nicky Winmar and Cathy Freeman and Nova Peris and any of Australia's remarkable Black athletes before her, Donnell Wallam carries the dead weight of our history. Like those athletes, she is lightened by the love of her people. I am sure that if you ask her, she will tell you that before anything else she is a First Nations person.

Donnell Wallam is being asked to celebrate genocide. Yes, that's what it comes down to. There is no smoothing this out or sidestepping it. Genocide. The extermination of a people. As the nation mourns the White Queen, some people – people with loud voices – seriously try to rationalise genocide. These people believe that a company bearing the name of someone who advocated wiping an entire people off the face of the Earth is fit to sponsor our national netball team. They believe, what's more, that this name should be emblazoned across the uniform of our national team. And that the only First Nations player in that team should wear the uniform bearing that name. For fifteen million dollars – the total value of the sponsorship, being three million per year for five years – the name Lang Hancock would be synonymous with the name Australia.

We should recall what Lang Hancock said. This man, who made his fortune from digging up and stripping the wealth from the land of First Nations people, saw us as a problem to be rid of. I search this man's name and find a video from 1984. In 1984, I remind myself, I am beginning my journalism career. I am twenty-one years old. This is not history. This is not something from the frontier that some might try to explain away as a reflection of a much less enlightened time. No, this is in my lifetime. This is from a man feted by the most powerful political leaders in the country. This is from a man of obscene wealth. This is from a man with murder in his heart.

Here is what he said.

'The ones who are no good to themselves, who can't accept things – the half-castes – and this is where most of the trouble comes; I would dope the water up so they were sterile and would breed themselves out in future and that would solve the problem.'

Solve the problem. He is talking about me and people like me. He is talking about Donnell Wallam. He is talking about Donnell's parents. Lang Hancock would rather that Donnell Wallam had never been born. She and I and everyone like us are a 'problem' to be rid of. He would poison the water so that we should die out. We 'half-castes'. We people of White and Black blood. We who are no good to ourselves, as he said, should be sterilised. And for this advocacy – of a genocidal solution to a 'problem' – this man paid no price. His company prospered. The mining leases continued. His wealth grew to obscene levels. And his company, Hancock Prospecting, could buy a national team. And a woman he would rather have exterminated was being told she should advertise his name.

Lang Hancock is long gone. But his daughter, Gina Rinehart, now runs the company that carries the Hancock name. She is by far Australia's richest woman. Her wealth has been estimated at thirty billion dollars. She is among the top 100 richest people in the world, due in large part to her father's legacy. That places her among the richest people to have ever walked this Earth. Donnell Wallam's protest presented Gina Rinehart a missed opportunity to publicly repudiate her father's vile words, to simply say 'he was wrong'. That didn't happen. And now, when Donnell Wallam refuses to wear the

Hancock name, it is not Gina Rinehart who is under pressure, it is Donnell.

In the weeks after the White Queen's death, Australia is seriously having a discussion trying to rationalise or justify genocide. Australian genocide is so nonchalant. The word is barely uttered. But what else could it be? Polish lawyer Raphael Lemkin developed the term in 1942 to describe the Nazis' systemic slaughter of Jewish people during the Holocaust. In 1951 the United Nations defined genocide as acts committed with intent to destroy, in whole or in part, a national, ethnic, racial or religious group. Included in the UN definition is 'imposing measures intended to prevent births within the group'. Genocide. That's what Lang Hancock proposed. To stop us breeding. To erase from the Earth people like Donnell Wallam; people like me.

In 1997 the *Bringing Them Home* report into the forced removal of First Nations children from their families laid this shocking truth at Australia's feet. There had been generations stolen. It had been planned. It was brutal. It was designed to break people, to sever the bond between parent and child. These stolen lives would lose their place in the world. The report found that Australia was guilty of 'systematic racial discrimination'. It was a violation of humanity. It was a violation of law. The report said Australia continued to practise forcible removal as official policy long after it was prohibited by international treaties. Treaties Australia had voluntarily signed up to. It was, in a word, genocide.

Now, in the weeks after the White Queen's death, I am listening to people of influence – people in the media, people running major national sports – defending the daughter of Lang Hancock more vigorously than they are defending Donnell Wallam. No, they say, Gina Rinehart does not have to reject her father's genocidal fantasies. No one, they say, is accountable for the actions of their parents. But what about us, we who have to live with what was done to our parents?

I keep asking myself: why should this be so hard? What does Gina Rinehart find so difficult about saying her father was wrong? No amount of money that she gives to sports or Indigenous organisations and communities – which she does, generously – can make up for her father wanting to sterilise us and breed us out. But in Australia anything is up for sale. We celebrate people who have systematically tried to wipe my people from the face of the Earth. We have statues honouring colonial figures who wanted to strike terror into Aboriginal people, who ordered the heads of Aboriginal people to be severed. We name suburbs and universities and buildings after White people who robbed others – Black people – of their land, who forced those people into segregated missions and reserves, and who locked them away behind laws that restricted every personal aspect of their lives. This is Australia. A nation that celebrates as its national day a day commemorating the invasion of my people's country.

Sometimes I think we are moving forward. I want to believe that we are laying the ghosts of the past to rest. In those moments I can even imagine a more just future for us – for all of us. But then I am reminded again of the simple, unalterable truth of Australia: racism is always forgiven. There is nothing that someone can inflict on us from which they will not be redeemed. Not even genocide. Hancock Prospecting underwrites our Olympic team. The name of a man who wanted us poisoned and bred out is synonymous with Australian sporting excellence.

When that sponsorship was announced, the then head of the Australian Olympic Committee, John Coates, said he was 'delighted' to partner with Hancock Prospecting. Coates boasted of how the committee was 'proudly independent of government'. But he was 'grateful' to have the support of Gina Rinehart. Coates was looking out for the interests of the Olympic team which supports First Nations athletes. Understandable. But it reminds us of what matters. Gina Rinehart's money puts her father's company at front and centre for the biggest sporting event in the world. At an Olympic

Games designed to celebrate peace, Australian athletes with gold medals around their necks publicly thank the daughter of a man who wanted to poison us.

Where is Australia's conscience? There it is, in the voice and the strength of one woman. It is Donnell Wallam who calls this out. One woman says no. Not the captains of industry. Not the captains of sport. And I wonder: where are our leaders? Where is the prime minister? He has led the mourning of the White Queen. He has declared a national holiday in her honour.

Donnell Wallam plays for Australia. She takes the court in the final quarter of the match against England. The game is in the balance, and Donnell Wallam steps up. With seconds remaining, she shoots for the match. Australia wins. No one is wearing the name of Lang Hancock.

❊

The White Queen is dead.

In the weeks after her death, I am standing in a packed room speaking to the top brass of the New South Wales police. It is not a comfortable place for me to be. Instinctively I distrust police. Why wouldn't I? These are the people who bulldozed my grandfather's tin home to the ground. They chained him to a tree like a dog. They beat my father senseless in a police cell in Sydney. I would watch them patrolling around where we lived. I was told, over and over, how they could take me at any time. Even now, if I see a police car, I tense up. If I see the police questioning Aboriginal people in the street, I watch. Sometimes I intervene. I see police two or three at a time with guns hanging from their hips standing over homeless people. Why? What threat do those people pose?

I know the truth: our jails are full of Black and Brown people. Poor people. Mentally ill people. People with drug addictions. I know that so many of our people are locked up for little things like unpaid fines. I know that mandatory sentencing laws in some states put children into jail for successive misdemeanours. I know that too many of my people go into police lock-ups and prison cells and never come out. They die there. Nearly five hundred deaths in the last thirty years. There are inquests and investigations, but never – not once – has a policeman been convicted for one of these deaths. I know that, in some states, every child in juvenile detention is Black. Every single one. What futures will they have? Even when they get out, what is there for them? And I know that I could have been them. That there were enough sliding doors moments in my childhood where I may have taken a different road. Where the door to my future would have been slammed shut.

So what am I doing here? Police Citizens Youth Clubs is raising money so it can keep programs going, to help keep kids off the street, to build trust among communities. There is hope here. I know how these things can change lives. I have seen Aboriginal communities and police working together to train kids, get them healthy, fill them with a nutritious breakfast and get them off to school. I have seen police arrests decline, I have seen crime rates drop, and I have seen something we do not see enough: Black kids and cops smiling at each other.

I grew up in these clubs. They were called Police Boys Clubs then. Every Tuesday night in my little town, I and other Black kids – my friends and cousins – would trek from the fringe of town, where we lived, to the club. We would learn how to box. We all wanted to be fighters. We would work the bags and the mitts. We would do sit-ups and push-ups. We would climb into the ring with headgear and mouthguards and circle each other. Those cops we would run from in the back streets we would now see in a different light. It didn't fix everything. Maybe very little, to be honest. How could it? Two hundred years of brutality can't be fixed on a Tuesday night. But it was something. It made us feel good. It made us feel tough and Black.

Now here I am, standing in front of the deputy police commissioner and the state governor at a plush Sydney hotel. There is goodwill in the room. I know the deputy commissioner – he's an honest man. When he was a district commander, he called me and asked if I would come and talk to his police cadets. I am here today because of people like him. I am here because of Aboriginal people in the room who are working to build better futures for Black kids. Rolling out training mats, pumping up balls, cutting up fruit, putting in long hours because they care. And I am here because of a little boy in Western Australia who no longer has a chance at life.

His name is Cassius Turvey. He was only fifteen years old. He had a cheeky, chubby face and a smile like a six-month-old baby. Innocent and seeking nothing but love. And he was killed, beaten to death while walking home with friends. Before he was attacked, he was subjected to racial slurs. Cassius was not the first. Sadly, I know he will not be the last. But his death at this time moved us. People were angry. They were heartbroken. Thousands held vigils across the country. Cassius would not be forgotten.

And he would not be forgotten in that room. When I walked to the lectern, I asked everyone to stand. I asked for a moment of silence to remember Cassius. I never knew him. But I wanted him – his memory – to be in that room. The commissioner of the Western Australian Police Force said Cassius had been in the wrong place at the wrong time. I wanted everyone in that room to know this: Cassius had a right to be wherever he wanted to be. Cassius had a right to walk the street in peace. Cassius was an Aboriginal boy and this land was his. We failed Cassius. We fail too many of our kids. This was an act of violence, but our nation is also born of violence.

Archie Roach, our beautiful Aboriginal singer, told us to be careful where we walked on this land because a child was born here. Children have been born here for two thousand generations. Our kids see things they should not see. Our kids die far too young. They take their own lives. We see images of our kids held down in police cells, sprayed with capsicum and pepper, with hoods on their heads, crying. I have had to teach my own kids that the police will not always be your friends. They have seen up close the worst of it. They have told me of being with their cousins and police taunting them. They have been stopped in the street. Their bags have been ripped from them and upturned, and they have been accused of stealing or of having drugs. Neither are true.

Still we hope. In the weeks after the White Queen's death, we are hoping. That's why I was in that room. And if we ever needed to see what hope is, what love is, it is then. We needed to remember Cassius Turvey. Forever fifteen.

And we needed to hear Cassius's mother. Mechelle Turvey takes pain and gives back love. That's what our people do.

What we have always done. What I was always taught to do. To give back love. Mechelle said we know racism exists, but she didn't want her son's life and death to become a campaign. Don't use my son's death to blow your trumpets, she said. She told our kids not to live in fear. Her boy wanted to be famous, she said. He wanted to get his name out there. His name won't be soon forgotten. Cassius Turvey.

For Mechelle Turvey, he will always be 'my baby boy. My miracle child.'

13

LOVE

The White Queen is dead.

It is dark outside. Still, silent and dark. There is the hum of the road. Headlights illuminate the edges, throwing just enough light for me to see where I am going. But I am transfixed by what lies just beyond the light. The hills and trees. The empty fields. Just as it always was. How I love driving at night. When I can lose myself. Alone, I can feel the Earth. And I know ... I know what is out there. Endlessness. Not time invented but time permanent. Time that does not run in a straight line. In my car, in the darkness there is life out there. All around me. We don't see it in the daylight. At night I can hear the murmur of old songs, of voices, of footfall. Eternity.

I see a boy in the back of a car huddled in with his brothers and sisters. It is me when I was young. It is night. It is always night. I look outside at the white fence posts as we pass by. This is the safest place in the world for me. Inside that car, nothing can touch us. The rest of the world is out there and in here there is us, a little family with no home except the one we have made together. For hours I watch my mother and father in the front seat. Silence mostly, the quiet broken by a soft word here or there. Dad sings to himself and keeps time by holding a bottle top and running it across the grooves of the steering wheel. He hands a packet of cigarettes to my mother; she takes one out and lights it, the red tinge piercing the darkness and shrouding her face as she takes a drag and passes it over. These are moments of love. Soft intimacies. Sometimes she reaches across and gently strokes the back of his neck.

This was the rhythm of my early life. My childhood was a blur of small towns. Each of my siblings was born in a different one. We were never in one place long enough to call anywhere home. Today we might say this was homelessness. Back then it was just life. It was all we knew. We bedded down in cars or by the side of the road. We lived in tiny gypsy caravans. Sometimes sawmill shacks. There was never a place to plant a garden, or pin a poster to a wall. Friends from that time are today mostly just a blur of faces, sometimes only a name. I was rarely in one place long enough for many to stick.

My heart aches for that boy. He is always with me. I am always there in those little towns. I feel sometimes as though I could close my eyes, open them and be back there. As if time has stood still. I can hear my grandfather coughing as he always did. His lungs were damaged when he was boy, and he was always gasping for breath or heaving up phlegm. I can see my mother making porridge. I can see myself toasting bread stuck on a long fork over an open fire. Dad has gone to the mill and my brothers are curled up next to each other in bed. The stone floor feels cold but there is warmth in the love in that little shack.

I have been around the world and back, and yet a part of me – maybe it is the truest and best part of me – has never left that time and place.

There's a song playing low in the car tonight. That song sounds so familiar. The sort of songs that sound tracked those long, dark drives of my childhood. Townes Van Zandt is singing about a love in a far-off place. Someone he lost. The sound of the fiddle sits just over my heart. Just where I keep my memories. This is music for long night drives. Yearning, reaching music. A bruised voice. Imperfect and cracked. And that's what makes it so beautiful.

Love. Just this evening, only weeks after the White Queen's death, I was talking about love. About hope. Hope and love in a world where those things can seem like false promises. But what else is there? Why else am I here? I was talking about love. I was hoping that the people in the room could find it in their hearts to love us too.

❋

The White Queen is dead.

The University of Canberra had asked me to deliver a keynote lecture in honour of its late vice-chancellor Don Aitkin. It was arranged months ago. If I had given it then, it might have been so different. I might have talked about politics. About history. About war. About the things I have seen as a journalist.

But the White Queen is dead. And tonight I want to talk about love.

Yindyamarra Winanganha. Say it. Feel those words on your tongue. What do you hear? Say it. Exhale. Breathe into the syllables. Yindyamarra. It is meant to be spoken softly. It is quiet. Like a prayer. Winanganha. These words hover. They float above us. What a people created these words. They are words that rustle through the leaves in the trees. Some of those people – my people – are in the room with me. My cousin Violet welcomes everyone to country. I watch her and I feel I am looking at our great-grandmother. There are other faces too. White faces. Unsure. Wanting to hear. But not knowing – not really – how to listen.

Yindyamarra Winanganha: to live with respect in a world worth living in.

'Who understands this language?' I ask. 'How can it be that a language as old as human time on this land has vanished?' I think about this a lot. Sometimes when I am home, I stand outside and look at the stars. Other times I sit by the river or the creek at dawn or dusk and I listen. I hear the rustling of wind in the trees. The sounds of birds. I think of how, for tens of thousands of years, these birds, these plants heard a sound. They heard a language. They spoke back to that language. Those birds are our animal spirits. My father's bird, the magpie – the garru. Forever they heard these words, and then they were gone. In just a blink of an eye, they fell silent. Do they miss those sounds? Do the birds miss us? Are they waiting still?

How can we speak to each other in this country when we don't speak the same language? This language was formed here. It gave name to everything around it. Wongamar. The name of my great-great-great-grandfather. He was here before

White people came. He saw his land taken. He saw his people killed. Budyaan – the dancing bird – my great-grandfather. He saw his language silenced.

My father – we know him as Stan Grant senior, Yemmaran Budhung – was only a little boy when he saw his grandfather Budyaan arrested for speaking our language. Budyaan called out to my father to come home and a policeman overheard him. Budyaan was accused of using offensive language and the cop took him to the lock-up. My father has never forgotten that moment. In that moment something entered my father – a spirit, a resolve that one day he would save his grandfather. His grandfather's words would be spoken again.

Dad's photo is on the screen behind me. It is the first photograph of my speech. I have chosen tonight the images of people who speak to the trouble in my soul. All my life I have asked the question: what do we do with catastrophe? It has taken me around the world. Everywhere I have gone, I have seen my father's eyes staring back at me. I am with him in this photo. One of the proudest days of his life. He is receiving a doctorate from Charles Sturt University for helping to save the language this country had tried to silence.

My father had to wait until his fifties for his grandfather to return to him. Dad had lived a hard life by then. His body is scarred with tattoos, broken bones and knife wounds. Such a hard man. He had to be. Life had no use for softness. Every day was a battle. Hard work. Little reward. Then a man entered his life. John Rudder was a linguist. He had worked with Indigenous communities in the Northern Territory, recording their languages. Now he wanted to see what could be salvaged of Wiradjuri.

John sought out Dad and they formed an unlikely friendship. Night after night, week after week, for months turning into years, they put this language down. They travelled across Wiradjuri country in southern and central New South Wales. Dad wanted to feel the language. Hear it where it was meant to be heard. Together they wrote the first Wiradjuri dictionary. What a thing of wonder. Never before, in tens of thousands of years, had these words been written down in this way. Now a new generation was learning to speak these words.

I remember standing with my father at the site of the old Bulgandramine mission. He is home. He is among the trees by the river. I am here early and I walk around. I see stumps on the ground, all that remain of the houses. There are old, rusted metal plates. I see a baby's cot, twisted and worn. People lived here: my people. My blood. I came across a booklet once, written by a local Wiradjuri woman, Rita Keed. She told stories about the old days. About how people laughed. Kids swimming in the river. About songs they sang. About the missionaries.

About sickness. About death. She listed some of the names of the people on the mission. There among them was Bill Grant. Next to his name were two words: 'the storyteller'. Bill Grant, my great-grandfather.

A group of Wiradjuri men have come here today to this old place to listen and to learn. They are awkward and uncomfortable. Probably embarrassed. They know they should speak this language. But they can't. Like their country, it was stolen from them. Dad starts to speak to them. He speaks to them in our language. These men repeat after him. They are soft at first. They shuffle and look down. I am standing off to one side, just watching. I know we are rolling back time. We are turning history on its head. After two centuries, we are alive. We know who we are. We have never stopped being who we are. And our language was always there, sleeping inside us. Now – here, today – all is right again.

When my father began to teach Wiradjuri, he offered our language to everyone. He wanted Black and White to speak it. So we could speak to each other. I asked him why. Because, he said, language is not about who you are, it is about where you are. And there, in that one simple sentence, is an entire world. There is Yindyamarra. The idea of the West – we could just as easily say the idea of Whiteness – is who you are. Identity. Individualism. These words that begin with the letter I. When

White men invented modernity, they sought to free us from everything that tethered us to the Earth. Religion. Family. Nation. We could live beyond it all in a universal world of freedom. Who you are is the most important idea of modernity. And it is a liberating idea. A view from nowhere. It can just the same be a view of nothing.

We humans may think we can float free in a world of perpetual peace. It tempts us to defy gravity. But we return to Earth; we return to the things that bind us. We form our tribes. And we go to war. Who you are may be the most dangerous idea in our world. Every war I have ever covered as a journalist is rooted in that one lethal question: *Who are you?*

But what about *Where are you?* That question asks us to look beyond ourselves. It turns us inward. And it pulls us into the Earth. Where you are. A language of this place. Words formed here and nowhere else. There are no walls here. There is no Black, no White. There is a place. There are people. And in this place, we meet one another. My father has always told me that any people who are in our land are our people. We must show them Yindyamarra. To those who have shown no love for us, we show love in return. Don't let them take that from us, he says. Don't let them take where you are.

I want the people here tonight to see my father's face. To look upon the face of this man who so honoured his grandfather. My father who helped to save a language; to save a people. If you ask him, Dad says he didn't do anything. His people did. His ancestors. Those men at Bulgandramine. The women who now run the Wiradjuri language program at Charles Sturt University. It is Wiradjuri women who are breathing life into our words. In these words we all find a language of love. We are speaking back to history with love.

✸

The White Queen is dead.

Behind me is the image of the White Queen. She is not from here. She does not speak the language of here. Her language is a language of somewhere else. It is English. Named for England. It is a language of staggering beauty. That is undeniable. It is the language of Shakespeare and Blake and Austen and Eliot and Melville. It is the language of Keats and Yeats. It is the language that Kate Bush and Joni Mitchell so tenderly caress in their astonishing songs. Joni, I too wish I had a river I could skate away on. But this language – this lovely language – has silenced so many others. It has become a language of who you are. Who the English deem us to be.

English silenced Gaelic. It took the tongue of the Irish. It stopped them speaking to stop them thinking. Silence is a weapon of war. A Welsh friend told me about the Welsh not – or the Welsh knot or the Welsh lump. It had many names, but its aim was the same: silence. Any child overheard speaking their language would be marked for ridicule. A piece of wood would be hung around the neck of the child. Into the wood was carved the initials W.N. – for *Welsh not*. Ask many Welsh today and they call this an act of genocide.

Words. How they define us. What we say is so often what we are. Our names. Our nations. Our anthems. Every word we speak inhales history. The Chinese writer Yiyun Li has said how she has tried to forget her own language. Chinese – *putonghua* – is just too painful. Too many memories. How she has tried to escape those words. Those sounds. Just as she has sought to escape her homeland. She has tried to take her own life, so much do those words of home hurt her. I asked her once: 'Is it gone now?' Not yet, she told me. But slowly she is becoming something other than Chinese. What? I am not sure she knows. Maybe nothing. Maybe she is seeking the ultimate home of modernity: nowhere. With words, with forgetting words, she says, she is committing suicide. She is killing the Chinese person inside her.

Here I am tonight speaking to these people in my language and in English. The truth is English is my first tongue. But it cannot be my mother tongue. The proclamations to steal our country were written in English. The orders to send out raiding parties to hunt my people down were written in English. It was in English that Governor Lachlan Macquarie gave his instructions to strike terror into the hearts of Aboriginal people. To hang Black bodies from the trees as a warning to all to submit to the Crown. It was a policeman acting in the name of the White Queen who arrested my father's grandfather.

I am not Yiyun Li. I am caught between words. In my soul there are words I still do not know. Wiradjuri words. From my mouth come the words that I am so familiar with. English words. Not my words but words imposed on me. I was asked once to describe myself; I said: 'I am a translator.' I am an act of translation. Translation is colonisation. Every translation is an act of betrayal.

❊

W.E.B. Du Bois looks over my shoulder. His piercing eyes stare out at the audience. He is another of those images I reach for. He was the one who told us that the twentieth century would be defined by the colour line. Tonight I want to tell people here about the veil. The veil of Whiteness. To let the words of Du Bois sit heavily in the room. He told us about the birth of his son. Born within the veil, 'and there within shall he live'.

Holding in his little head 'the unbowed pride of a hunted race'. Du Bois said in that moment his son grasped, in his tiny, dimpled hand, hope. But Black hope. As he said: 'A hope not hopeless but unhopeful.'

Has anyone else spoken so tenderly of hope? A child born into a world that has already decided his fate. And yet his fate is to push against fate. Born into a world stripped of hope. Unhopeful. Yet in the face of that, he does not surrender to hopelessness. What, I wonder, did my mother or my father or my grandparents have to be hopeful about? People say silly things like hard work is its own reward. Hard work left my father tired and still hungry. It left my mother's hands red raw from washing cars to earn extra money. But in spite of it, they were not hopeless.

I wonder if I am as gracious. As courageous. In spite of their lesson to me. In spite of the lives of virtue they have lived, I know I can turn sour. History, it is true, has poisoned me. It is a bitter taste. As Shakespeare wrote, time is out of joint. That's why I follow ghosts. Derrida warned us about this. He asked: 'What does it mean to follow a ghost?' And what if we are the ones being followed, 'always persecuted by the very chase we are leading'? Then, he said, 'the future comes back in advance: from the past …'

✻

Friedrich Nietzsche gave name to this: *ressentiment*. I return again and again to this poisoned chalice of history. Because I have drunk from it and vengeance is in my bloodstream too. It becomes the source of identity. The 'man of *ressentiment*', Nietzsche said, has an unquenchable thirst for revenge. He is caught in a time warp. A prisoner of his past. Always returning to the wounds of history. Always returning to the source of injustice, which he cannot fix and does not want to fix.

Czesław Miłosz called this the memory of wounds. And without justice, there is no hope for healing. And there is no justice for the immense crimes that have been committed here. How could there be? So now the image of Nietzsche – his crazed gaze – appears behind me. It is like he knows me. He knows my resentment. To me, his has always been a disturbing vision. A world without god. Where we have erased the horizon. He despised the morality of the weak. He saw the superman – the *Übermensch* – as the fulfilment of the triumph of the will. And we know where his ideas can lead. The likes of Hitler, who have found inspiration in Nietzsche's godless utopia.

But is Nietszche right about *ressentiment*? Hitler was consumed by it. Vengeful for the humiliation of the defeat in the First World War. Resentful at the Treaty of Versailles, which took German land and imposed economic cost for the war. This wound festered. He never wanted it healed. He wanted revenge. Resentment is so seductive. Evil is a seed planted in a potter's field, the graveyard of the unknown. And there it grows. Unblessed. Demagogues and despots know that this wound can be the source of their power. They deal in victimhood. And history tells us the levels of depravity people will go to once they fall under the sway of evil.

Adolf Hitler is always the outlier. He is the far marker of depravity. The Holocaust is horror beyond imagining. Except it breeds in the warped imagination. Evil can so often beget evil. And the victim today can be the perpetrator tomorrow. Amartya Sen has lived through this. He was a boy when his country split apart – partition between India and Pakistan. At its heart was faith and identity: Muslim and Hindu. And today the two nations remain locked in a lethal nuclear-armed stand-off. This is the solitarist identity Sen saw up close. The worst of identity.

Identity can shrink our world. It can reduce us to one simple thing: race, faith, culture, and nation. Identity can set fire to the world. These are identities that kill. They kill with abandon. Every conflict I have covered is rooted in solitarist identity. At the core is history. Not events. Not time. But the stories that live on inside us after events and time have faded. The Vietnamese novelist Viet Thanh Nguyen once said all wars are fought twice: first on the battlefield and then in memory. Yes. And we who have memories of war are always counting the dead.

✸

The White Queen is dead.

Her image has now passed into history. What happened during her reign. What happened before her under the Crown. These things are in me. I can't wish them away. They are the wars we fought on the battlefield and the wars I now fight in my memory. Some wonder why this matters so much. Things happen, they say. They happen to all people. No one today should be responsible for the things of the past. The sins of the fathers and mothers. I am often asked: *Why can't you move on?* People who ask me don't realise what they are saying. There is a universe between us in that question. *Move on.* There, in two words, is what the West – what Whiteness – is. Time runs in a straight line. History is shed like old clothes.

Why can't I move on? What if I don't want to?

I know why the West is so tempted by amnesia. I know why forgetting is so prized. Because the past is too ugly to look upon. While ever there is the past, there can be no peace. Horrible things have happened in the West. The worst wars in humanity have been fought among the tribes of Europe. Revolution. Plunder. Starvation. Out of this slaughterhouse was always the promise of utopia. That's the liberal dream. That we can resist our worst instincts. That we can illuminate the darkness. Beyond the guillotine and the gulag was the light of peace. But it is distant light. There is always the next war. These dreams die in the death camps. And the survivors are marked with tattooed numbers and a pledge: *Never again.*

Theodor Adorno asked: how can we write poetry after Auschwitz? He's right, isn't he? Words are not enough. They will always fail to describe that last breath. That last murdered breath. Poetry could just be betrayal. To reach for transcendence or beauty would feel obscene, as if the deaths of millions were just inspiration. What about words to capture the horror? Angry words. Sad words. Will they do? Can we write a poetry of resistance and remembrance? Perhaps. But we already have those searing images, those faces gaunt and staring, to tell us more than words can.

Adorno was warning us that poetry can tempt us to hope. And hope can be the mocking fulfilment of the Enlightenment. The promise that things will be better. We can move on. Poetry would be enlightenment's gift to the victims, and Adorno wanted us to know that enlightenment was the reason we had the horror. Holocaust and hope are enlightenment's twins.

The ancient Greeks told us to be wary of this hope. The story of Pandora, who opens the box holding the evils of our world. Sickness and death escape. When she closes the box, hope is what is left inside. It may seem a comfort. But maybe we are reading it wrong and hope is a deception. Hope is the blessing withheld. It stays behind while evil has its way. To some, hope itself is one of the evils. To Hesiod, hope was the gods' reminder to us that we must suffer. Hesiod warned that hope was for the lazy mind. Nietzsche read hope as the most evil of evils, because it prolongs our torment.

If poetry was hope, then surely it died – surely it must have died – in Auschwitz. Jean Améry, who was born Hanns Chaim Mayer and lived through the death camp, would not let hope dim the memory of those he saw die around him. These things would not become footnotes in history. Améry saw his resentment as a virtue. It was what he owed to those who did not survive. Is that not the debt I owe too – that I should never let hope absolve the perpetrator? Hope doesn't come naturally to me. I am torn between hope and vengeance. Hope dwells among the stars and can feel just as out of reach.

Here is another image behind me. The *Angelus Novus*, the Angel of History. It is a childlike artwork, an angel with wings outstretched, created by Paul Klee. The German-Jewish writer Walter Benjamin bought it for a thousand marks in Munich in

1921. It became his talisman. It never left him. He hung it on the wall of every home he lived in. It spoke to something he'd been grasping for. What was history? How could we explain the hold the past has on us? Here it was, in this image. Benjamin wrote that the Angel's eyes are staring wide, his mouth open. The Angel's head is turned backwards, towards the past. The chain of events merge into one single catastrophe and the wreckage piles at the Angel's feet. The Angel stares into the abyss and the abyss stares back.

Is this me? Are my eyes like the eyes of the Angel of history, always turned to the past, to the abyss? Am I like Adorno, unable to imagine poetry after apocalypse? Does Hesiod's myth poison hope for me? Okay. It feels good. It feels worthy. It feels righteous. But it doesn't feel true. Truth was the love I felt in that car, snuggled in with my brothers and sister and quietly watching my parents. What other proof did I need of hope, of love, than what I saw inside that car?

Walter Benjamin took his Angel of History with him to Paris when he fled the Nazis. He would flee again and take his own life before the war's end. Jean Améry survived the war but fought it forever in his mind. His resentment was honourable. His words can still speak to me. Because of him and others like him, we can never forget. But Améry could never forget either. And he was tormented. Where there was no hope, there was no tomorrow for him. Jean Améry who as Hans Chaim Maier lived through the horror of Auschwitz, took his own life in a Salzburg hotel room in 1978.

❖

The White Queen is dead.

There is an old American Indian fable. It tells of the old woman in the afterlife. When warriors die, they meet her at the gates of paradise. The woman eats the scars off the bodies of the warriors and they are cleansed. For those without scars, the woman eats out their eyes. It is through our scars, our wounds, that we heal. We can only truly see through pain. Those without pain are blind. They are blind to truth.

I want to tell the people here tonight about how we can still find hope in catastrophe. The hope – the radical hope – is etched in the face of an American Indian man. A Crow chief. His name was Alaxchiiaahush. Of the great warriors of the Crow, he was the greatest. The Crow – known to themselves as Absaroka – were the most feared warriors of all. They lived for battle. Everything they did was preparing for war. When a Crow mother cooked a meal for her child, she was building strength for battle. Sleep and dreams were a prelude to war. When a Crow warrior entered battle, he would ride into the centre of the plain and plant in the ground his coup stick, daring the enemy to meet him. Beyond here, he was saying, no one must come. You will not penetrate my land, my soul. That would be worse than death itself. With each victory, the warrior would take a trophy to tie to the coup stick. Alaxchiiaahush took more coups than any other. He was known for it, and remembered as Chief Plenty Coups.

The Crow Nation's great enemy were the Sioux. They feared the Sioux would overrun Crow land. They had battled White invaders, and then they joined with the White people to fight the Sioux. The Crow were moved onto reservations. Promised lands were reduced time and again. Disease and hunger wiped out up to a third of the surviving Crow. The life they had known is over. The land is not theirs to define or defend. To plant a coup stick and dare the enemy no longer has any meaning. Life itself has become unintelligible.

I discovered the story of Chief Plenty Coups in a book by Jonathan Lear. Plenty Coups knew catastrophe. For him, time passed with the passing of the buffalo, which were wiped from the plains as surely as the White invaders erased the Indian people. When the buffalo died, he said, his people's hearts fell to the ground and they could not lift them up again. Then Plenty Coups said something that haunted Jonathan Lear: Plenty Coups said that after the buffalo, nothing happened. It sounds like the end of history. But what could it mean, Lear wondered, for history to exhaust itself?

This is not simply depression. Sadness. It is not something peculiar to Chief Plenty Coups or the Crow. There is something shared here. Something that binds our humanity. If time can cease to exist for the Crow, so it can for us all. Then we must ask: what comes next? How do we live with this? The question is not just 'How can I go on?' but 'How can I go on as a Crow?' How do we write poetry after apocalypse? For the Crow, for Chief Plenty Coups, it would come in a dream.

Alaxchiiaahush was a young boy when in a dream he saw the future. It was a world changed. He saw the buffalo gone. And he saw himself. Unrecognisable to the young Plenty Coups. He saw himself old. He saw himself in defeat. And, in the dream, where all was lost he saw the chickadee, the smallest bird, not strong but wise. The chickadee said power comes from the mind, not the body. Alaxchiiaahush's dream allowed the Crow not just to glimpse the future but to prepare for it.

Plenty Coups knew that if his people were to survive, if their hearts could be lifted again, they would have to find a new way to fight. Courage is not just fighting but knowing how to fight. As Jonathan Lear learned from the story of Chief Plenty Coups, courage means knowing what is shameful. To lose hope is shameful. To feast on resentment is shameful. In a world collapsing, Alaxchiiaahush would not give in to the shameful. There is life on the other side of the abyss. Not just survival, but flourishing. The Crow would use their minds. They would, as much as possible, hold on to their lands.

As an old man, Plenty Coups visited Washington DC to mark the burial of the 'unknown soldier'. He represented the Native Americans who had served in the First World War. He wore his feathered war bonnet and carried his coup stick, and laid both down with the sarcophagus. He was burying them – a ceremony to mark the passing of a time and a life. It was the end of a tradition and the beginning of new ritual.

Something here still disturbs me. Is it surrender? It's certainly a moment tinged with sadness. But there's courage, too. It's a virtue as old as Plato and Aristotle. They pondered the living of a 'good life'. To have a 'good spirit', the essence of happiness. It is not a state of being – it demands action. It's a way of being in the world. With his symbolic burial, the Crow chief posed a question: how does a courageous people make a transition to a new world – to a new way of being? The old ways of war no longer defined life on the reservation. Yet the way of the warrior need not die.

Plenty Coups asked his people to face a new culture with openness and willingness to learn – to find strength in wisdom, like the chickadee of his dream. Here is Jonathan Lear's notion of 'radical hope' – that is, hope even as a people experience catastrophe. It asks: what can legitimately be hoped for when all meaning and certainty has gone?

There are echoes of this in the story of the Wiradjuri people of western New South Wales – my father's people. After the crossing of the Blue Mountains, they fought the British, who declared martial law and slaughtered the Wiradjuri population. After years of battle, the Wiradjuri leader, Windradyne, walked what remained of his people over the mountains to meet Governor Thomas Brisbane. He wore a straw hat. Written on the brim was the word 'peace'. His radical hope. Not surrender, but renewal. His straw hat, like Plenty Coups' war bonnet.

I hear an echo of Alaxchiiaahush in my great-grandfather Budyaan. He tells his grandson, my father, that he must find a new way to fight. They will go into the bush and they will dance and talk. And that language, and the spirit of the birds, will enter my father. Those words lived in my father until the time came to speak them again. And this is in me. It is what rescues me from resentment. It is what speaks to the poetry in my soul.

❉

The White Queen is dead. I am hearing the voices of those who have spoken back to empire.

Now it is the voice of the Canadian Indian singer Buffy Sainte-Marie. I remember her from my childhood. I saw her on *Sesame Street*, an Indigenous woman who spoke to me then as a child. Now I hear her again, speaking across time in a podcast. It is an interview from the 1970s and Buffy is trying to explain how her people suffer still. How Canada is a nation diminished by its treatment of Indigenous people. She is talking about truth. And the hope that Canadians will finally hear the truth. But the interviewer is hearing only anger.

To the interviewer, when Buffy talks about the war against her people, she is talking about vengeance. Because that is all the interviewer can hear, or wants to hear. She misses Buffy's joy. The joyful things she sings about. The things that give her hope.

The interviewer tells Buffy how she should feel. She believes Canadians are becoming more aware of the Indian plight and that Buffy is being churlish. It's as if Buffy is not entitled to her anger. Canadians, like Australians, are always on a journey of understanding. They give it various names: *integration, assimilation, reconciliation.* But for First Nations people, there is always the threat of annihilation. That's what Buffy Sainte-Marie is trying to tell the interviewer.

They each have their own version of hope. The interviewer has the White hope of progress. Buffy has our hope, a hope full of love. Love that is tested and loves in spite of history. They can't communicate even when they're talking about the same thing.

Buffy Sainte-Marie sang for the Queen. She sang of when the buffalo died. How her people had been mistreated and wronged. Of treaties broken again and again. And how she was told it is all in the past – how she should forget and move on. But it still keeps happening. Now that the buffalo is gone. She sang for the Queen. So the Queen knew. She had always known.

Now the White Queen is dead. I am here with the words of Buffy Sainte-Marie, the words of my father. The words of Du Bois and Plenty Coups. So many words, so many faces. Some are Black, some are White. These names and faces that are my inspiration. That challenge me. Songs and stories. It is through words that I make sense of the world. And with words I speak back. Sometimes angry, sometimes sad. Sometimes with hope, sometimes without. But through it all there is the word *love*. The face to which I turn next knew the power of love. She knew the strength of faith and what it was to walk with God. Truly walk with God.

❋

Simone Weil looks so tiny. So frail. Thin and gaunt. Her skin alabaster. She is birdlike – just like Plenty Coups' chickadee. Small and wise. She did not live a long life. She died in 1943, at only thirty-four years old. She was stricken with illness most of her life. Struggling with tuberculosis, exiled in England after fleeing the Nazi occupation of her native France, Simone refused food in solidarity with those suffering back home.

Simone had always stood with the afflicted. With the forsaken. For a time she turned her back on scholarship and worked alongside people in a factory. When she was only six years old, it is said, she refused sugar because she would take nothing more than the troops fighting on the front lines of the First World War. She wrote widely, forever defending the rights of the poor and downtrodden.

Simone was many things: philosopher, activist, fighter. It is Simone the mystic who has inspired me. She said that God entered her body when she heard villagers sing hymns in a church in Portugal. She said she first kneeled to God in a church where Saint Francis of Assisi prayed. She never joined a church. Her congregation were the people outside the church doors. Hers was the Christ of the forsaken. Not for her the vision in White. She felt the power of the Christ on the cross. Beaten, bedraggled. His was not a glorious death but a shameful one. He was humiliated. In that moment God had left him. Simone Weil says that is true for us all. In our movement of despair, we can feel abandoned. A kind of horror submerges the soul, she said. In that darkness the soul ceases to love. But love lives on in the emptiness. We go on wanting to love.

I know that. I know that loss and abandonment, and I know that love. The love that endures. The love that is bigger than death. I first felt that love in a little church of my own. It was the little white wooden church on the Three Ways Aboriginal reserve – the mission, we called it – in my home town of Griffith. Some of my earliest memories are there. Squeezed into the pews, my uncle preaching the sermon, all hellfire and spit. Mopping the sweat from his brow with a handkerchief. He could preach without notes for what felt like hours. Making each point by stabbing with his finger, and it always seemed to land on me.

We held ourselves together there. We shared our sorrows and pooled our hopes. As a boy, I sat in awe and fear. I knew, in that place, that we were in a battle between good and evil. I fidgeted and squirmed and looked around. I would often feel ill and leave the church with a blinding headache. Yet I felt, even at that young age, a power. Call it a spirit. It was real and it was personal.

That church was a haven. Men and women would turn out in their Sunday best: long dresses and pressed white shirts, with their Bibles – well thumbed and marked – tucked tightly to their breasts. We would strum guitars and sing hymns. Afterwards we would eat sandwiches and drink cordial. I would run free through the mission fields, burrs in my feet, and swim in the irrigation channel. In my mind I can take myself back there. Back to that little old church on the mission. Me with my spit-down hair, and around me all the people I would call my own.

I remember the night the old church burned down. I watched from our kitchen window as the flames reached into the sky. I looked on in a trembling fear. Like a great sin was being committed. It was as though I were a witness to the crucifixion itself. God's house ablaze. It was shocking and yet – I could not deny it – also powerful, symbolic: a reckoning. Burn it all down. All of our history, all of our suffering, the great injustice of Australia: burn it all down. Wasn't the Church itself complicit in the whole bloody mess of colonisation?

Why would we look to a Christian god? Isn't this the faith of the coloniser? Didn't those who brought the Bible also bring the gun?

Yes.

The missionaries came to 'civilise' us. Our lands were stolen and we were herded onto reserves. On one of the missions that my family was from – Warangesda, on the banks of the Murrumbidgee River – the missionary John Brown Gribble would hunt people down if they tried to flee. He would ride after them, tie them up and drag them back. To Gribble, the outside world was a living hell. He wanted to save us, but in saving us he brought his own tyranny.

Gribble called himself a man of God. But where was God for us?

Ours was the church of the afflicted. It was in our abandonment that we found hope. That we found love. Simone Weil said it is only the afflicted who know truth. The truth in that little church was love. All that remains when everything else departs. Our little church of the forsaken. The voices of my people, especially the women, my aunties soaring above all, singing of an old rugged cross, the emblem of suffering and shame. We would have had every reason to turn cold in our shame. In our abandonment to seethe with resentment. But we were warmed in that little church, warmed by a love. Love. All that we had left.

I have seen this love wherever I have met the forsaken. I have seen it in the faces of refugees fleeing war. I have seen it in mothers who have had to bury their own children. Call it god. Call it spirit. Call it human. But it is love. My Buddhist friend and teacher Tonglam radiates love. My dear friends

Zeeshan and Dildar, devout in their Islamic faith, offer nothing but love. Between my Baha'i friend Farhad and me there is an enduring love. I have found this among peoples of all faiths. And it is the same love that I felt first in that little church.

As we watched the old church ablaze, my father just shook his head. All he could say was thank God his father – my grandfather – was not around to see it. I don't know what caused the fire. Probably a kid messing around. Whatever happened, it burned down a memory. A blessed memory.

❅

The White Queen is dead.

Love. I reach for an image of love that I can show these people before me tonight. And here it is. Uluru. The heart of our nation. The place where our people gathered to offer words of love to our country. These people who had come from all points of the southern sky to ask Australians to walk with us for a better future. These people spoke of the torment of powerlessness. Of how our children languish in detention centres. Of how too many of our people die far too young. These were the voices of the forsaken. And above it all, they spoke of love.

The Uluru Statement from the Heart is a gift of love. A gift from those who have walked the hardest road with the heaviest burden, but have never sunk so low as to lose our love. For what is left without love? That's what comes from our Earth. It is what I feel when I go home. It is my ancestors beating in my heart. What greater testament to love has existed in our nation than this? That we must love those who have committed the greatest sin on us.

Miroslav Volf is a man who knows about love and forgiveness, who lived and suffered through the wars of Yugoslavia. He knows the bitter hatred that exists between Serb and Croat. He was once asked if he could embrace a Serbian. In spite of all the conflict and hatred, could he forgive? No, he said. But then he said he must. And it starts with knowing we are each morally divided. There is a rot deep in our souls, a prowling beast of exclusion. This inhumanity gave Whiteness its divine purpose in the first place. It allowed the horrors of invasion and genocide. But when do we say stop? When do we forgive? Forgiveness is not absolution. Forgiveness is earned. And if my people offer their forgiveness, the perpetrators must face what they have done. We must embrace, across our history, across our pain – because in that embrace, Volf tells us, is the struggle for the truth of humanity.

The Uluru Statement is a testament to love and forgiveness and truth. It is a testament to hope, even as we approach hope with caution. When hope can be a false god. But I know to lose my hope would be shameful. It is not what I was raised for. If I think only of myself I can feel hopeless, but if I think of others I cannot. It would be a sin to remove hope from a world already hopeless. My ancestors would be ashamed of me.

❖

Someone asks me if the referendum will be successful to put a First Nations Voice to Parliament into the Australian Constitution. This is what the Uluru Statement calls for: Voice. Treaty. Truth. That there should be justice. That in a land stolen from us, we may finally be heard. That there should be truth.

Australia has tried to hide from its past. But my people know the truth. We were invaded, our ancestors were shot, poisoned, decapitated, and raped. We were excluded, segregated and locked into missions and reserves where it was assumed we would die out. Can a nation with such a dark history be redeemed? Are some things beyond forgiveness? My faith tells me we should forgive those as we ourselves seek forgiveness. But God also says there is eternal sin. There are crimes against man and then there are crimes against God. God dies where his people die. God died in the gas chambers of Auschwitz. God died in exterminating wars against Native Americans.

And God died here in the Frontier Wars against my people. These are crimes against God. These are eternal sins.

Modernity has supplanted God with its own faith in progress and reason. The liberalism that emerged out of the seventeenth- and eighteenth-century Enlightenment imagines that we can wash ourselves clean of the past. But there can be no redemption without atonement. The Voice walks this line between justice and forgiveness. It risks becoming captured by the liberalism it seeks to speak back to. For me the Voice must speak from the right side of God. It must speak from the side of suffering.

The political battlelines have been drawn. In November 2022, on the day I gave the Doug Aitkin Memorial Lecture in Canberra, one side of politics announced it had rejected the Uluru Statement. It is not surprising. It has been rejected before. We have grown so used to rejection. This nation – the shameful, dishonourable part of our nation – has never been able to face what it has done.

Australian liberalism has never had a place for us. Any future for us would be on Australian terms. There are people now for whom the idea of a First Nations Voice is an affront to Australian values. Listen to the way Australians talk about us, like we are a conquered people. Well, we are not. We are talked about as if we are not there. They speak as if Australia is settled, and it is for them. Yes, some say we should be better. But to them, Australia is a fact, and we are told we should accept it. We should be absorbed into the Commonwealth, just as the old assimilation policy decreed. Australia has not really moved that far from assimilation.

Even some people who say they support us lecture us that we should be modest. They say we should not ask for too much. Some say we should not call the Voice a First Nations Voice because that would be divisive. As if stealing someone's country was not divisive, as if living in a nation that has never acknowledged our true place, our true sovereignty, a nation with no treaties, is not divisive. Others ask, should Indigenous people have rights that no other Australian has? Why, they ask, should race be in the Australian Constitution?

These questions are inane. As if Australia is not already defined by race. There has always been a race power in the Australian Constitution, and it has always been used against us. And here they are – these people who imagine a world beyond race – defining us still by race. I do not belong to any race other than the human race. But I belong to a people. That's what we are: a people of this land. We are a people who truly could come from no other place. But call it race if you must – the fact remains that this is our land. Time matters, and our belonging here is eternal.

The Australian Constitution does not tell us who we are. How could it? My constitution is written on the land; I carry it inside me. I did not need an axe to fell a tree to break the silence, to make my home here. A Voice to Parliament embedded in the Constitution can never amount to justice. We know that. But there are rules. There is governance. Such mundane things, yes. But by these things our lives are determined. So a Voice to Parliament asks that we can advise and have input into policy directed towards us. Simple, isn't it? The prime minister says it is a voice, nothing more, nothing less. He is telling us more than he realises. After two centuries, this is what we get: nothing more, nothing less. Just a voice. It will always be less than we deserve, but all we can expect. The best we can hope is that it may help keep us alive.

I am not here to speak of politics. Politics feels cheap to me. Whenever I come close to politics, I feel diminished. Mere politics cannot ease the depths of our affliction. Politics alone cannot deliver justice. So why a Voice? If the Voice means that our people can live longer, healthier; if it means our children have a chance to walk in this world as who they are, then it is critical. These are things for be fought for. There are political battles to win. But the Uluru Statement from the Heart is bigger than politics. It is even bigger than the Voice. It is love.

And if we cannot find in ourselves love for our place, and for each other, what future is there?

This talk of love may seem dreamy. It may seem naive amid the cut and thrust of political debate. And the person who asked me the question wanted from me a political answer. He wanted me to denounce Australia. He wanted me to be angry. And yes, I can do that. I understand the urgency of anger. I understand why people would want to upend statues. I understand why they may want to burn an Australian flag. Let those statues fall I say, but I also know that those things seem so small next to love. Bell Hooks said we have been 'wounded in the places where we would know love'. But still we look for love. As she saw it, love is 'profoundly political', and only love can 'give us the strength to go forward in the midst of heartbreak and misery.'

Oh, how reading Bell Hooks deepened my understanding about the transformative power of love. As she spoke of the African American experience it spoke to me too. We know the love of heartbreak. Bell Hooks said money won't save us. Black people thinking capitalism will save us fail to understand the spiritual depths of our crisis. Black militant struggle, however righteous, also lost sight of love. She said the 'denigration of love in Black experience ... has become the breeding ground for nihilism.' Our love has to spread its arms around our communities. We hold each other tight. I know that my people's love, my family's love lives in me always and I will honour that by refusing to surrender our fight for dignity and justice. Our love for each other; for our country; and yes, even for those who have done us wrong, is not love as weakness. That love has saved a language and saved a people. Politics didn't do that; love did that.

Politics can steal hope. It seems to me too often a grubby business more akin to accounting than leading. Not that sometimes a politician does not aim higher in words at least if not in deeds. But most politicians are unnecessary. Truly, has there ever been a politician who does not disappoint us? Politics is about what is possible, and that will never be enough. For my people, there is no voice loud enough to speak back to all that has been done to us. But love rescues us from politics. My prayer is that one day with enough love in their hearts those who sing the songs of the glory of Australia will find love enough for us too. Until then, I look to my people, my memories and love. Tell me this: has there been a politics strong enough to bear the weight of love in that little white wooden church on the mission?

❊

The White Queen is dead.

My mother and father are old now. Their battles have been fought; some lost and some won. They have been wounded by Australia. But they are still here. I watch them sometimes when they are asleep, just as I watched them when I was a boy from the back seat of the car. I watched my mother tenderly stroke the back of my father's neck on those long, dark nights. I watch them now. Their hands are together. Two people lost in their dreams and in each other.

In their sleep, they make the world so clear to me. All these questions I ask – these things that tear at my soul. Can I forgive? Can I put aside resentment? Can I keep speaking to people who cannot or will not hear? And in that moment – maybe only just for that moment – I have my answer in two people at rest in a world that they have made out of nothing but love and hope.

14

BETRAYED

The White Queen is dead.

I spend my life talking. To so many millions of people here in Australia and around the world, I am a face to varying degrees familiar. I have been talking publicly for so long that to many my voice is recognisable. Television, radio – these are intimate technologies. I can seem like I am right there in your room or in your ear.

Strange that this should be me. As a boy, I barely wanted to speak. In school I would shuffle to the rear of the classroom. I moved around so much, attended so many schools, that I felt like a phantom. There one minute and gone the next. I even loved the *Phantom* comics, of the masked man in Africa. Vague and mysterious. At home I would often be in a quiet corner reading whatever I could. Wandering around the backyard or the street, lost in my own head. Sitting in trees, daydreaming. How could I end up on television when I never even wanted my photo taken? There are barely any images of me as a child, and not one I can readily remember where it was just me. If I am there at all, I am with family, somewhere off to the side.

The White Queen is dead.

Here again I am off to the side. I don't want to speak. I won't bring my voice, my face, to this moment. I cannot – I will not – put on a black suit, a white shirt and a black tie and join this ritual mourning. It isn't disrespect; I respect what the Queen meant to so many. I respect their sadness. I respect her as a human being; burdened, flawed, loving and loved, like us all. It is the White Queen I cannot mourn.

It is the White Queen as an idea. It is what that idea means. What that idea has done to my people, and to people like us everywhere. I cannot mourn that. To mourn that would be betrayal, and I won't betray the memories of my forebears. I won't betray my grandfather, whose breath I can still feel. Even in death. I won't betray them by mourning the White Queen.

But I feel betrayed. Right now, in the hours after her death, I am betrayed by people I think of as friends. I am betrayed by colleagues. I am betrayed by the place that I work. I am betrayed by my country.

In the early hours of the morning, I am sitting in an airport lounge. Every television is switched to the news. Sombre faces and voices pitched soft, and everyone dressed in black. Like everyone, I am processing what has happened. Everything moves so quickly in our world now. News comes at us from all angles. What would once have spread gradually across our world now pings instantly from every phone.

We used to wait for history; now history happens in a flash. There is no time for consideration. Posterity is not counted off in generations but measured in memes and tweets. Hot takes pass for analysis. A blog takes the place of an essay. Everyone is a journalist. Every phone is a camera and a recording studio. Expertise is valued in speed as much as in insight, if not more. So it is now. Every reporter, every analyst, trying to capture lightning in a bottle. Filling minutes that will stretch into hours and days and weeks. I am of this world but it feels dizzying to me at this moment. It is ludicrous. And I am furious.

A breakfast television news host tells us that she met the White Queen. The host is White too. She says the White Queen had an aura. Only a matter of hours after the announcement of the White Queen's death and this news presenter has nothing left to say. What she is describing is not real. It is the figment of an excited White imagination. She has nothing of value to add. If she knew any better, she would not say even this. She would not say that this woman was ordinary. That, stripped of the jewels and crowns and castles, she was one of us. Stripped of all the loot of war and empire, that is; all the wages of sin.

That's the difference between the Queen whom I met – pleasant, practised and polite – and the imagined White Queen. Real is not good enough for this White television host. Not now. She needs to create a White myth. So the White Queen is beatified. She has an aura, just like the halo around the imagined White Christ.

I can't blame the White news presenter. What else would she do? Hundreds of years of Whiteness has told her that she is special. Almost everyone around her is White too. All the television news hosts speaking from every corner of the airport lounge are White too. The greatest gift this news presenter ever received was her Whiteness. More than her talent. More than her hard work. All real, I'm sure. But it is her Whiteness that assures her place in the world. I wonder how many people not White have been passed over so that this White news presenter can tell us how special the White Queen was. I wonder if the White news presenter ever pauses to think about that.

White people are always special to White people. Was Elvis Presley truly the King of Rock'n'roll? Everything he did was in imitation of Blackness. But to White people, he made it acceptable. He made it human. Sam Phillips, the record producer who discovered him, knew this. Give me a White boy who sounds Black, he said, and I will make a million dollars. Elvis was a Goldilocks act – not too much, just enough. Little Richard was more dangerous. Chuck Berry smarter. Al Green had more soul. Ike Turner had more menace. But Elvis is crowned the King: he had an aura.

White people always have an aura. Did you know that of the 954 people who have received Nobel Prizes, just seventeen have been Black? It is true. That is fewer than 2 per cent of all Nobel laureates. Twelve of the Black laureates have been awarded the peace prize. Not recognised for intellect, science, economics or words, but peace. Black people trying to bring peace to a world of violence that Whiteness visited on them.

All these thoughts are running through my head as I sit in the airport lounge and the golden dusk is breaking around me. I feel hurt and the anger keeps building. Until anger turns to sadness.

❖

The White Queen is dead.

It is Friday night one week later, and I feel like I am dying. I have sharp pains in my chest. I am anxious. It is midnight and I am lying on my bed, willing myself to stay awake. If I close my eyes, I am afraid I won't wake up. Downstairs, my wife is working. Should I call out to her? I need to go to hospital. *Breathe*, I tell myself. *Calm down*. I am having a panic attack. We might think it is all in the mind, but it is physical. It is as real as a punch in the stomach. Now I am winded and I cannot catch my breath.

I have been here before. I know this. I have known this all my life. The truth is I have been gasping for air since I was a boy. Since that time I became conscious of the world into which I had been born. I cannot say there was a moment – one moment – when the world appeared clearly to me: it came to me, as I'm sure it came to you, in flickering images. Here I am at five years old, dressed in a pressed white shirt and dark shorts and holding my sister's hand. She has a little skirt on and an innocent smile. No doubt these were the cleanest, nicest clothes we had at that time. Our Sunday best to go to church.

'Jesus loves me, this I know ...'

This is the first trick. The world offers a vision of beauty. A vision so pure. And it tells us this is love.

How could I not fall in love with the light-haired, blue-eyed vision of innocence? That radiance. The long, flowing locks, arms outstretched, his head shrouded in a halo. The White Jesus. The Jesus sent to save us. My sister and I with our soft Brown skin.

My life is captured in snapshots stored in my mind. Family. Being at the river. Curled up in the sun. Lying flat on concrete. I have snapshots of the most beautiful place on Earth and I have never been able to properly breathe here. I have never stopped running. Now I feel like that kid again. I felt like this all the time back then. A knot in my stomach. Racked with fear. Worried about everything and everyone. I worried that my father would die. I would curl up against the window and look down the road for the dust from his car. Proof that he was coming home. That he had survived another day at the mill.

The mill was a dangerous place. He had already lost the tips of his fingers. When he came home, he would be covered in sweat and sap and blood. But he was home at least. The mill could kill him – and then where would we be? Who would take care of us?

The mill was dangerous but Australia was worse. Australia was lethal. It stalked my dad from the day he was born. It was coming for him like it came for his fathers and mothers before him. It had already broken Dad's bones and bruised his soul. It made him hard and remote. It robbed life from him.

And it took a bit of my father from me. The father he would have been, or could have been, if he wasn't so tired and so sad. And that sadness was part of my inheritance. It was taking life from me.

Now the White Queen is dead and I feel like I am dying from Australia. Its betrayal is killing me. And we know how we die hard here. We have been dying hard here for two centuries. Two centuries of life under the Crown. Two hundred years and we die ten years younger than other Australians.

There's a town where some of my grandmother's people live. A town by a river, surrounded by fertile ground. The type of place where Australia was built and grew rich. Not far from this town, the oldest human remains in Australia were found. More than forty thousand years old. The man was estimated to have been in his seventies. Today Aboriginal men in this town have a life expectancy of less than forty.

Australia, you never cease to find new ways to break my heart.

*

I have not been able to catch my breath since I heard the news the White Queen had died. It was hardly a surprise – she was an old woman, ninety-six years old. Not even her wealth and privilege could conquer death. The news network I work for, the Australian Broadcasting Corporation, had plans in place just for this eventuality. Everything choreographed. The right dress code. The right tone of voice. Nothing left to chance. The

ABC being the ABC, a White person would bring us the news, because White people mostly bring us the news at the ABC. White people are the faces of the ABC from morning to night, on television and radio.

In the days after the White Queen's death, I have stayed off the air. Ordinarily I would be on screen for hours. At the ABC I have broadcast elections, wars, crises of all kinds. These are the moments I have lived for as a journalist. For two decades I travelled the world. I reported from more than eighty countries. I called London, Islamabad, Abu Dhabi, Dubai, Hong Kong and Beijing home. I know enough of New York or Paris or Shanghai or Cairo to feel at home there too. I worked for many years for CNN, the American news giant. There too I covered wars and natural disasters and revolutions. I spoke to refugees, killers and presidents. There is nothing more satisfying than matching my talent, experience, knowledge to big events. Yes, it is ego, but that alone is not enough. When I am exhausted, mentally shattered, hungry and crying, what keeps me going is service. The hope that what I am doing does some good in the world. But not this time.

I was asked. Within hours of the White Queen's death, a television producer called to ask if I would present the coverage that evening. It would be on prime time, when most people would be watching. No, I told him. I was being asked to participate in my own betrayal. I knew what this would be. This would be an assault of Whiteness. And it was. Hour after hour. White people interviewing White people about the White Queen. This is what the media does: it frames the narrative. It sets the parameters of discussion. Everyone followed the script. They spoke of the White Queen's grace. Her service. Her duty. The tough times she weathered. They spoke of her over and over and over. None of them knew her, but in death they were creating her.

At moments like these we are reminded of who we are. Who we truly are or what truly matters. There is a story Australians like to tell about themselves. Australians can be good in a crisis. In flood and fire, people find hitherto unknown strength, courage and kindness. Yes, this is all true. In this we are laudable, but not remarkable. I have seen the same thing everywhere. Even more, in many places. When people are tested, stripped of fortune and hubris, their humanity – the beating heart of survival – always shines.

Nowhere is this more visible than in refugees. Carrying all they have left, with no way of turning back, clutching their children, they go on. They are fleeing violence and famine and tyranny. Look closely, trace the lines of their fate, and you can see the hand of power. You will find Whiteness. Sometimes it is hidden. Faint. Often the refugees – Black and Brown – are fleeing people who look like them. But keep going, keep looking: Whiteness is there. Always there, hovering somewhere.

Whiteness has drawn borders, installed dictators, exploited resources – and paid off its agents. It has created this world the refugees are fleeing from, and then it gets to decide who lives or dies. Rich White nations decide who is worthy of their mercy. In Australia, we know to our shame how we turn people away. We lock them in detention centres. We drive to insanity desperate people already on the brink of madness. Our nation, forged in invasion and colonisation, pledged for much of its history to the ideal of Whiteness. A country which sealed itself behind a White Australia policy. Now it finds new ways to exclude the Black, Brown and poor.

❖

The White Queen is dead.

Who are we? It is no surprise. We are White. Obsequiously, unashamedly White. Nowhere is this truer than at the Australian Broadcasting Corporation. My own organisation is White to its core. The chair of the organisation is White. Has only ever been White. The managing director is White, always White. The director of news is White. The executive producers of the news programs are White. From morning to night, the faces on the screen are overwhelmingly White. The senior reporters, the presenters of news programs, the people who bring us our politics and guide our understanding of the world. On federal election night in 2022, the ABC decided that an all-White panel – five White people – would explain it to the nation. In an election where more diverse candidates were successful than at any other in our history, the ABC was White. White, White, White. Yes, there are a few of us, non-White sprinkled through. And slowly it is changing; too slowly. We remain the exceptions that prove the rule.

I am one of those exceptions. I have breached the wall. And I can tell you, it is a lonely, tiring and maddening place to be. There is no honour in being a 'first'. It doesn't speak to opportunity or progress. It speaks to intransigence, bigotry, low expectations. White people see our success as their achievement. Look how good we are! Look what we have done!

When the ABC appointed Bridget Brennan to its London bureau, it congratulated itself that she was the first Aboriginal person in the organisation to be a foreign correspondent. Shame. Bridget deserves better than that. She is not their creation. The organisation did her no favour. What she is she has earned. But the hidden message – barely hidden – is that we should be grateful.

I walked into newsrooms as a young man all alone. No one was like me. There was no one who had walked my road. No one I could look at and in an instant understand. No one who shared my history. People who laughed like me. In those newsrooms, my people were laughed at. Journalists would put on mocking Aboriginal accents. When they talked about us, they talked down to us. Not all – there were those who supported me, and I thank them. But I knew I was in a battle to survive. I had to pick my fights, and suck up the daily indignities to win the bigger battle.

What has changed? In forty years, have we left racism behind? No. There are people on our screens who have been guilty of racism. They have apologised for 'getting their words wrong'. But they pay no lasting penalty. They are rewarded.

I am watching television one morning. Watching a White reporter at an event to celebrate women the world over. Especially to recognise those who suffer and struggle. She is at a breakfast. I can see so many White faces and there are Brown faces too, mostly wearing aprons and carrying trays of food. Serving White people. Each hour the presenters cross to the reporter, and each hour she speaks only to people who look like her. The most oppressed, brutalised women in the world are the women of colour. But she speaks to none. I wonder if her White eye see others as equally human? Is that unkind?

Perhaps. But we – people who are not White – are so regularly overlooked. Only White voices are heard.

I call one of our news bosses to complain. How is this acceptable? He agrees. He says there is no place for casual racism. Casual racism? Only a White person could call racism 'casual'. That's what Whiteness does. It controls language. It gives racism a name, then diminishes it. *Casual.* Try this: *micro-aggressions.* Another invented White term. It is used to describe the daily slights, the humiliations that we non-White people experience. But the word makes them small. Trivial. What are we really talking about? Next thing they are saying it is all in our minds. I tune in a few weeks later and the White reporter is on my screen again, speaking to Australians who look like her.

In the weeks before the White Queen dies, the head of ABC News issues a statement telling us what we people who are not White already know. The ABC is not a safe place for us. It is racist. He expresses his sorrow about this.

He is a good man. I have no doubt he is sincere. I have had conversations about racism with him and I know he is committed to change. But he is also trapped in the logic of Whiteness. The statement says all the things all racist organisations say: we will not allow or tolerate any racism in the workplace. Ever. But the ABC does. Even after this statement, the racism continues. Aboriginal staff tell me that racist comments from their colleagues actually *increased* after the news boss's statement.

One man, not White, tells me he doesn't feel as though he belongs at the ABC. He says he just tries to fit in. I know what he means. I don't belong either. I work here. I have friends and colleagues whose company I enjoy. I am proud of much that we do. But I keep my distance too. I keep a space like a forcefield around me so they don't get too close. Do I truly belong? No. The ABC isn't mine. Not like it is theirs.

If I fool myself I belong, I am soon reminded that I do not. Now that the White Queen is dead, they are telling me who this organisation truly belongs to. I am reminded whose lives matter most. The White Queen's life matters more than the lives of all others. The ABC's coverage is anaemic.

Think of what we could have done. We could have thrown open the doors and created a crescendo, a discordant choir of anger, sadness, tears, love, respect, disrespect, regard, disregard. We could have invited a reckoning with history, but instead we erased it.

No one stands with me. I know, right now, that I am alone. My people do not matter. Here, in this moment of the White Queen's death, we do not matter. That's the truth. How could it be other? Not one of the White journalists says no. Not one says this isn't right. Not one thinks of my people, before the

White Queen, before themselves. Not one considers how I might feel. And if they do, even for just a moment, they make their choice. They put on black suits. And I don't hold it against them. I find an excuse for them. I remind myself that they are doing their jobs. They are like the White Queen, doing their duty. They are good people. But they are not my people. Not at that moment.

Why do I stay? Why wouldn't I? I deserve to be here. I have worked for this. This is my country, and my people have been pushed out for too long. When I came in to journalism I made a pact with myself that I would not be anyone's idea of what an Aboriginal journalist should be. I wouldn't be pushed into a corner. I wouldn't do the 'Aboriginal stories'. What are they, anyway? Doesn't the economy affect us too? Don't healthcare, education, employment and defence affect us too? I wanted to tell the stories of our world. I wanted to talk about China, Russia, the Middle East, and the United States. I wanted to bring my eye, my perspective, to the bigger issues of our time.

Today, there are still so few of us. White voices and White perspectives are prized most. They are the experts. Throughout the world, we who are not White outnumber them nine to one. But in television land, they have all the answers.

I have sat in meetings where White people talk about us right in front of us, as though we don't exist. They always know what is best for us. In one meeting, a White man talks freely about how the White audience on an ABC program laughed at a Black singer. They thought he was a joke.

I am listening to this. These words coming out of this White man's mouth – about the mockery of a Black man – hit me in the gut. It feels like an assault. He says he didn't mean anything by it. He didn't mean to upset me. Maybe. He just can't control what comes out of his mouth. Like so many White people, he does not know when to shut up.

These things happen every day, in every workplace across the country. In every school. In shopping malls, on sporting fields. Everywhere. All the time. My sons tell me how they check themselves. They stay away from certain places. They avoid White crowds. They especially avoid drunk White people. Because they know what to expect. Not that it will happen every time. But it can. Even in the most innocent – seemingly innocent – ways.

I am sitting with a friend. He is Indian-Australian. We are having a coffee at an outside table at a cafe. A man recognises me from television. He comes over. He is pleasant. He says he likes my work. He says he is surprised to see me. Then he looks at me, studies me. 'You're darker than I thought,' he says. That's what matters to him. That's what he notices.

It is a violation. He is invading me. My skin is my skin. It is not for him to study. To question. But he knows he has the right to do it. And there is a judgement in his voice. I have heard this so many times. I know what too often comes next. 'How Aboriginal are you?' 'But you're different – you're not like the others.'

They invent Whiteness. They inflict it on us. They get to decide. Then they judge us.

The ABC is racist. Of course it is. Racism is not what White people do. It is what we – non-White people – see. But so often, apologies are to those of us who have 'experienced' racism. As if this is only something *we* feel.

The statement from the head of ABC news comes after an internal report. We told them what was happening. Is that what it takes? That they must hear it from us? Are they wilfully ignorant? I wonder why they can't see it for themselves. The report was written by a diversity committee. We have to investigate. We have to bear our pain. We have to open their eyes.

Even in the apology there is redemption. White people are always redeemed. The ABC says it is employing more diverse people. More Indigenous journalists. But the ABC – Australia – is two decades behind the rest of the world. Whatever their own racism, in other places I have lived, people like me are not invisible. At CNN or the BBC or Al Jazeera I have been in news meetings where people like me are the majority. If there are White people there, they know enough not to presume that their voices will be the loudest. But the ABC – just like Australia – is always striving to do better. And that is meant to be enough. That is meant to be celebrated.

So here I am. Behind enemy lines. I have infiltrated the citadel. I look around and there are still so few with me. At the ABC I am the only Aboriginal person permanently presenting a primetime nightly news or current affairs program. After ninety years, this is what the ABC has to show for itself.

The ABC did not create me. I was lucky. Doors opened that I could never have anticipated. A world appeared to me. I wonder why. Yes, I work hard. I know we have to be twice – three times, ten times – as good. Timing has been part of it. Those before me have blown down the walls. And there is something else, something that makes me cringe. I am acceptable. I am Black enough without being too much. Just enough for White people to feel good but not threatened.

That's the deal. But I will make it count. I will not make it comfortable for Whiteness. I will not be another brick in the monument of their greatness. I will not put on a black suit and tie. I will not lower my voice, bend my knee, bow my head to the White Queen. Not now.

If you had asked me a week before the White Queen died, I might have answered differently. I might have imagined that I could go on air, speak dispassionately. But now – now it is real. Now the White Queen is dead and I can feel my ancestors surging inside me. I know what is right, and this – what I am seeing on my screen – is not right.

There are some people of colour at the ABC – people of countries colonised by the Crown – who do wear black. They do join the coverage. I can't speak to that. Perhaps they have made their own peace, their own accommodations. They are outnumbered; maybe they feel compelled – I don't know. But I do know I will not be a part of this, and I know that I am doing the right thing.

❧

The White Queen is dead.

The ABC has set the tone. It is not the right time. The angry voices. The righteous voices from the other side of history should be kept quiet. Australian political leaders, from the prime minister down, are on air reminding us to have respect. What does that mean? It means they would rather talk about corgis than colonisation. The White Queen's love of her dogs matters more than the lives of those that the Crown has broken. The ABC spends the first night of the mourning period talking about how many magazines the White Queen sold. How she was good for business. Everybody's grandmother, we are told. Let me say it again – not mine.

There is no place for anger. Unfiltered anger. If we appear at all, it is to be understanding, understated. Or we too might cry for the dead White Queen. I see one Aboriginal man. A proud, defiant man. A leader who has been a champion of peace and reconciliation. His life has traced our journey for justice. He has led that journey. Now he is telling us about the time he met the White Queen. He took a delegation of Aboriginal people to London. To the palace. He walked through the imposing gates. Past the Union flag and the Beefeater guards. He told of how he sat with her. And I see tears in his eyes. She was kind, he said. She listened. For the first time, he said, he felt like a White person was treating him as a human being.

It is to her credit. This is the Queen – the blood and flesh human being. The Queen with a heart. Not the Queen as an idea. Not the White Queen. He was meeting a human being like himself. But he returned to a country where the White Queen rules. He returned to a place where his skin has been a crime. A death sentence.

Watching him, I start to cry myself. What had this country done to him? I know what he is saying. I have felt that too, that gratitude. It comes from some place where I don't think I am worthy. He sounds to me like the beaten child looking always for the parent's love. I know that too. The wounded child who sees a glimpse of kindness and thinks it is love.

❖

I have a friend, a White friend. We work together at the ABC. But we are more than colleagues. In many ways, it is one of life's unlikely friendships. We come from such different places – we are such different people. The White friend was born in the city and I am the child of too many small towns to count. The White friend grew up in working-class comfort with a foot on the ladder of respectability and a pathway to privilege. I, a Black boy, lived a life of chance. No amount of hard work or hope alone would ever be enough.

I have seen people work hard – Black people – toiling in the blazing sun picking fruit or labouring in sawmills and abattoirs. I have seen people – Black people – bend their backs for little more than a meagre meal. This was my mother and father. I know how their hard work was often never enough. Hard work was no guarantee of anything. Call it luck, as that's the only thing to call it – that's what made the difference in my life. Luck beats hard work. My fate was as random as throwing sixes on a roll of the dice. I got lucky, and somehow my White friend and I found each other.

We carry ourselves differently through the world. He is buttoned down and more likely to be wearing baggy corduroy and soft loafers. I will be in jeans and sneakers or chinos and boots. I can see him in tweeds, meandering in the English countryside. He was born for mist and village greens. He belongs in a Constable painting.

Maybe that's the bond between us, the Black boy and his White friend. He is a man of values, not fashion, and tradition matters to him. Those things matter to me too. And his dreams of a far-off White land he was not born in are no different to my dreams of my land.

We share lunches and talk of books and ideas. We share faith, although we each come to God in our own way. The White friend knows stately churches of stone and liturgies of incense and sonorous hymns. I know a white wooden church and sweat and the strum of a guitar joined by lilting, soaring voices. Black voices. They sing songs less of praise than of pain. But together my White friend and I, the Black boy, find a way to communicate.

But not now. Now there is a world between us. Now his Whiteness has come between us.

The White friend told me he had shed a tear for the death of the White Queen, and I could not understand that. Not that he had shed a tear for someone he had never met – I have done that. I remember when the musician Kurt Cobain died, and the personal sense of loss overwhelmed me. I knew Kurt had lived a painful life, and in that moment I felt all of that pain. Something in his pain touched something in my own. But my friend's grief for the White Queen felt like a betrayal.

How could he call me a friend and cry for the Crown? That Crown had stolen my land, slaughtered my people, imprisoned us and sentenced us to generations of poverty? I had spoken so many times to my friend – my White friend – about these things. Now he cries for the White Queen.

What, I wonder, was he crying for? I have heard so many other people say the same thing. An ABC radio host – another person I consider a friend, someone with a sharp, inquiring mind and a quick wit, someone well travelled and equally well read – said on air how he was surprised at how emotionally overwhelmed he became when he heard the news the White Queen had died. He was fussing about the house, getting breakfast, preparing his children for the day ahead, rushing to get out of the house on time, and there he was in his kitchen blubbering, he said. He was still wondering: what was that all about? He did not consider himself a royalist, but he was crying for the death of a remote old White Queen.

I understand sadness. I have known a deep well of sadness all my life: it is a sadness that comes from an aching in the land itself. I am one of those people who absorb the sadness of others around me. Sadness never leaves me. I balance it with moments of joy – a walk, music, books, the smell of jasmine or cut grass on a summer day, a bee frothing in the wattle, the touch of my wife's hand, the sounds of my children's voices, the memory of my grandfather. I am grateful, though, for my sadness. It is precious. It reminds me I am human and I feel.

But I am numb to the sadness of my friend. Yes, I feel betrayed by it. It is the worst betrayal – White betrayal. This White betrayal falls silent when someone makes a racist joke; this White betrayal puts self-preservation above justice or decency; this White betrayal is comfortable. White people know when they have betrayed us. They know the times when they have opened their mouths to object, to speak up, and then swallowed their words. They know the times they have been in a football crowd and heard racist abuse and just lowered their heads. They have kindly uncles who say 'embarrassing' things. They have racist friends who remain their friends in spite of their racism. Because Whiteness excuses itself. Whiteness justifies Whiteness. And White people know that they can always find refuge in their Whiteness.

Whiteness cries for its own reflection. And so now it cries for the White Queen. That's the grief of my White friend, and the radio host so surprised by his own emotion. And it is unforgivable to me. This Whiteness is unforgivable. As much as I might tell myself I must forgive. Right then at that time forgiveness is beyond me.

My White friend is hurt that I am hurt. Something has shifted between us. I can feel it. He can feel it too. And I can see it on his face. There is pain there. Pain that I am rejecting him and I am rejecting what he believes in. And he is right in that. Our friendship is strong enough to survive this. But at that moment he does not feel like my friend – he is every White person. Yes, he is the good White person. But they are capable of betrayal too.

These good White people tell us they share our pain, they ask us to walk with them, they stand by our side, and sometimes – sometimes – these good White people die for us. I know the good White people. They come to me sometimes and tell me how ashamed they are of their Whiteness. They are ashamed of their history. Then they ask me what can they do to help? It is an impossible question for me to answer. What they are really asking for is absolution, and I cannot offer that.

That's what they want from my friendship: they want to be absolved. That's why they ask me what can they do for us?

But they are asking the wrong question. And it does not occur to them that they are asking the wrong question. They should not be asking me what they can do for us. They should be asking what they can do for themselves. What civilisation is it that gives the world mass murderers that can invent the gulag and the gas chamber? What civilisation is it that needs to invent Black people, and then enslave those people and strip those people of all they own and crush the skulls of those people? What is that need? There is nothing they can do to help me. There is nothing I can do to absolve them.

Now my friend is crying for the White Queen. And I want to say something to hurt him.

❋

The White Queen is dead.

It is six days now. I have yet to appear on air. But I am about to. My program is looming. Every week on *Q+A*, we open the room to voices we don't often hear. We give the microphone to people to speak back to power. They provide the questions. A panel of so-called experts – still too often White – give the answers.

I have been thinking about this all week. I am conscious – always conscious – that I am alone. There is no one else at the ABC like me. After dark, the ABC is almost entirely White. I am an Aboriginal person in White Australian lounge rooms. Most Australians still say they have never met a First Nations person. Few can say they have Aboriginal friends. Real friends. People they have in their homes. Share meals with. Spend Christmas with. And here I am, talking to them about things they are not used to people like me talking about. Some hate it. I have seen the audience research. I have read how at least one in ten viewers don't like me – in their words – running my 'Aboriginal agenda'. I know what they are really saying. They don't like who I am.

Now, as Australia mourns their White Queen, I am going to be talking to them when many would rather I shut up. I won't be wearing black. I will not silence the sharpest tongues. The ABC is nervous. It has circled around these topics all week. The republic. Colonisation. Empire. Genocide. Racism. If they've been discussed, it has been in muted tones. No one wanting to step outside the lines. At one point it is suggested to me that *Q+A* might not discuss the Queen's death at all. One producer suggests we do a program on aged care.

That would be ridiculous. No. We will do it, I say, and I will put Black voices front and centre. And Black women. My friend Sisonke Msimang – the South African writer – and the Wiradjuri lawyer Teela Reid agree to be part of the program. They know what to expect too. They know that among the praise and support there will be hate. They will be targeted. So will their families. They will be accused of being victims. They will be told to get over it. All the things we have heard so many times before. And because, in the media, we feel compelled to bring balance, we invite a conservative defender of the monarchy. Someone who clings to the virtue of empire.

Balance can be an absurd notion. Where is balance in our world? Where is balance in brutality? In crimes against humanity? We – whose people have, in many cases, lost everything – cannot speak truth without someone else speaking back to us. I am not going to name the White former politician who was invited onto the program to defend the Crown. If anyone cares, they can look it up. I won't name him because they always have names; people who are not White are so often nameless.

At times like this, my role is impossible. As journalists, we cling to our objectivity. But that is a lie. Who is objective? What a bloodless idea. There is nothing objective about the way my people – my family – have been treated. And what is objective about this ritual mourning of the White Queen? I am expected to ask the questions. To give the guests 'equal time'.

To make sure all voices are heard. As if truth can be divided and weighed. At other times I can step back, try to be neutral. Tonight I find my anger rising. Afterwards, some people say they could see it on my face. Yes. Of course they could.

The White politician talks about 'ugly scenes' in our history. That's right. Invading someone else's country, importing disease, shooting defenceless people, cutting off heads, dismembering bodies. These are 'ugly scenes'. (The next line is usually that 'it could have been worse'. As if we were lucky that it was the British stalking us and not the French or the Dutch or any of the other White empires. The British, we are usually told, were 'enlightened'.) What was happening in the eighteenth century, as these men of the Enlightenment were talking about truth and justice and freedom? When they were setting the parameters of what it means to be human, they were also measuring Black skulls. They were questioning our intelligence. They were wondering whether we had souls. They were debating whether we were human at all.

This man in front of me says: 'to say ... all of the issues ... should be laid at the feet of the Crown, rather than individuals who perpetrated some of the ugly scenes within Australian history ... King George III did not seek to invade Australia, but ... to settle it, and ... in the letters patent to Governor

Arthur Phillip said that he should seek to get the friendship of the ... as they were called then, the natives ... And so, were there skirmishes? Were there massacres? Yes. Were they perpetrated by the Crown? No. They were perpetrated by individuals who disregarded the letters patent ...'

As he speaks, I can feel the veins tightening in my temple. There were wars fought on our soil. Soldiers under the Crown were dispatched to kill us. Vigilante groups were formed to round us up. To force us over cliffs. To set fire to our homes. To lace our food with poison. But no, to this man – this defender of the Crown: 'if people misbehaved, so be it, and they should be brought to account. But to lay all the blame at the Crown is ... just flies in the face of the objective, documented history.'

I can feel my heart pounding. Sisonke and Teela answer back at him. I can't tell you what they say, as I am not hearing them. My people were slaughtered. Martial law was declared against my people. That meant the law was put aside. It was suspended. No one would be arrested for killing us. At the time, everyone in this colony knew it was a war. The newspaper called the battle for Bathurst – as it was known – an exterminating war. Every face in front of me disappears, and I am seeing my father, my mother, cousins, uncles and aunties. I am seeing the people I love. There is so much love for the White Queen. There is so little love for us.

Whiteness is not White people. I have to keep reminding myself of that. It is an organising principle. It is a way of ordering the world. It is an invention. An idea. A curse. Yes, there are people who want to believe they are White who cling to Whiteness. But this night there are White people on the panel who are appalled. They challenge the White politician. One of them is a friend of mine. We have shared dinners. We are fascinated by ideas. We are enthralled by philosophy and ethics. We can talk for hours. On this night, after the program, he looks at me with sadness. 'How can you sit there and hear that stuff?' he asks.

The truth is I can't. It is cruel. It hurts me. I wonder: what am I doing here? I have wondered that throughout the news coverage of the dead White Queen. I can never accept this. This is a moment of history. This is a time to decide who we are. I thought – I had hoped – that we were something else. Foolish me. I had so often looked to the best of this country. I have earned the ire of my own people at times for being too generous. Too forgiving. And I will always be forgiving. I will always respond with love. I will always prefer kindness. That is the gift of my ancestors. But I am sorely tested now. I feel wounded. I feel empty. I just want to go home.

✻

The night after, I am lying on my bed. My heart is racing. I am struggling for breath. I really feel like I am dying.

Who rescues me? My people. I can feel them with me. I can feel my grandfather next to me. I can hear my father speaking our language. My mother's words are ringing out across time. From a time when she was young. When she wore her brother's cast-off socks to see the White Queen. When she lived in a tin humpy with a White mother and a Black father. When broken biscuits made her cry. I can feel them, and I write. It is their voices that speak to me. It is their words that fall onto the page. It is their voices that matter.

You have read this. Right at the start of this book, you read their words. You heard their voices. I needed to start there, because before you heard me, you needed to hear them.

Back then, when the mourning is at its peak and I am struggling to breathe, I wonder whether the ABC will publish it. It does. But I find out later how the ABC editors struggled with it. They debated whether I had crossed the line. They discussed whether what I was saying had strayed from analysis to opinion. Analysis. Opinion. Cowards' words. Journalism words. Words that strip my truth.

My mother's life is not an opinion. History is an opinion. Whiteness is an opinion. My mother – my sweet, gentle mother – is a human being. The White editors of the ABC are doing what White people in power have done for centuries. They are measuring her humanity. They are weighing her life on the flimsy scales of their editorial policy. The White editors of the ABC may as well say she cannot be trusted. I cannot be trusted. Our truth is too heavy for them now. They publish it and hold their breath.

What the White editors don't know is that Australia is ready for this. All week, throughout its coverage, the ABC has failed to speak to the nation. Not all of it. Not the many people of this nation who look in the mirror and do not see what the ABC sees. These people are looking beyond Whiteness. They are looking at a nation of possibility. They see a human pinwheel of colours and cultures and languages and faiths. A new people tossed together, finding each other, loving each other. Out of this we are creating a nation. A nation that is still to come.

The article I write becomes the most read article of the ABC's entire coverage of the White Queen's death. What were they so afraid of? All week the ABC has not wanted to step out of line, and yet it has been out of step with the people it is meant to serve. I had feared a backlash. I had worried that my family, my parents, would be targeted. The trolls of the Twitter sewer might assault them. And yes, it happens. These people don't like us. They despise who we are. But in this moment other voices speak louder. They give me hope.

At the ABC, some of my colleagues – those who had willingly, or even just dutifully, bowed their heads to the White Queen – contact me. What broke in me has broken in them too. They send messages of love and support. I feel a weight lift. All of this I have carried. This that has taken my breath away. I can share it now.

This is why I am here. This is why I would not wear black. So that I can stay true to those gentle people. My family. Those small voices buried under the noise of empire. So they can be heard. And they are heard. Above the blare of trumpets, the marching feet of soldiers, the royal carriages, the cacophony of White voices spinning the myths of duty and service and aura – they are heard. And those who I wasn't sure even cared – they are listening.

Writing this is hard. So hard. My soul feels heavy. I am standing in the morning sunlight, letting its warmth hug my body. The sun in my face never fails to lift my spirits. For tens of thousands of years it has risen on my land. It has warmed the skin of my ancestors. Whenever I need them, they are there.

Now, when I am feeling low, my heart heavy, my phone pings with a message. It is from my oldest friend. My brother Ditchie. That's what we call Richard Bamblett. We grew up together. We were Aboriginal boys from the fringes of town. His family and mine wind around each other. We share blood.

We can recall when we stood in the principal's office in high school with other Black boys and were told that we would amount to nothing. The principal was wrong.

I left and began a journey around the world that has brought me back to where I started. Ditchie stayed. He raised a family. His children have gone to university and are beginning their own trek through the world. He has worked tirelessly for our people. His town. His community. He still has the same beaming smile and bear hug. When I think of my friend there are words that immediately come to mind: steadfast, loyal, and strong. But those words are not big enough to do him justice. Ditchie is loving. Always loving.

I don't talk to Ditchie every day, but he is never far from my thoughts. And I am never far from his. This day he messages me to ask if I am okay. He tells me he is thinking about me. Just when I need him, he is there. Across time and space we can read each other's minds. We can feel what the other feels. We can sense our souls.

15

WIRAY NGIYANG. WIRAY MAYINYI.

The White Queen is dead.

In a White land far away, the church bells are muffled. Ninety-six times they faintly toll, one for each year of the White Queen's life. In this White land, they know this day as D-day. Each day from now until the White Queen is laid to rest will be known as D+1, D+2 and on and on.

Radio stations are notified by a blue flashing light. Only music from prepared playlists will now be allowed in this White land. Newsreaders will wear black suits and black ties in this White land. And they will read from specially written scripts. A White King now stands over the coffin of his mother, the White Queen, and bows his head. And the people of this

White land bow theirs. For they are prepared for this; it has been rehearsed down to the minute, to the second. Where to stand. What to wear. Every moment choreographed. Feet fall with precision.

These people know their place. When to fall silent. Flags are being lowered and gunfire will salute the White Queen's life. For this is how things are done: dead monarchs are saluted with weapons of violence. They call it ceremonial gunfire. But so many millions of people around the world know there's nothing ceremonial about this gunfire. My own people know that. Those guns were turned on us and countless others just like us.

More than two centuries ago, the White Queen's third great-grandfather, a White King, sent a White Sailor to my people's land with instructions to cultivate an alliance with us and annex our country for the Crown. The White Sailor had not set foot on our soil before he fired his guns on us. Blood was spilled before a British flag was raised. And the people from whom they stole – my people – were now subjects of a faraway White land. And so we remain to this day, and we have never been recompensed. There is no bill of sale.

The White Sailor knew he needed only to plant a flag to claim an entire continent for a White King on the other side of the world. In this way, on violence and theft, Whiteness built an empire. This tiny speck on the map ruled over countless millions of people – at one point a quarter of the land on the planet – and the people of the empire boasted that the sun never set on their dominion. What was plundered was passed down the royal line to the White Queen now dead. And it has passed now to a White King, and there is another White King in waiting who will inherit what was stolen.

You could say it is all tradition. Strip bare the ceremony, the flag and the anthem and what remains? The White land is a land invented. A land imagined. A land dreamed. It is a land with its own story, written by its own romantic poets. White poets. A White land bestowed by the Almighty, where feet in ancient time walked upon mountains green, and was the holy Lamb of God on pleasant pastures seen.

White Kings and White Queens have been farewelled from this life for centuries. But Whiteness never dies. On and on it goes. One White monarch followed by another White monarch. A symbol of White purity and innocence. For this is what Whiteness is. It is why the virgin bride wears white. Why Catholic popes and Shinto priests wear white. We are baptised in white. Evil deeds are cleansed in white.

Now a new White King will be blessed with holy oil. A gift from God. As if God would place hands on this man and no other. This is how Whiteness is made divine.

❊

The White Queen is dead.

Oh, how beautiful this place is.

I am sitting watching the river flow. The current moving swiftly. Green lily pads carpet the water. Willows bend and kiss the riverbanks. There are dead logs and broken branches and tufts of grass, and there right in front of me I see it: a perfectly formed scar on a tree that for thousands of years people – the people whose blood I share – stripped for canoes. I paddle out on this river whenever I am back. I lose myself. It is as if two centuries have never happened. It is so alive here. All the distractions and noise fall away and I can hear … really hear. A curlew is calling. Frogs croak. A dog barks far off in the distance. I can even hear the insects. The crickets. There's a butterfly flitting in and out of the flowers, bringing beauty to creation.

I love rivers. I like the ocean, but I love rivers. Oceans seem violent to me; the waters in a rage. Oceans are the waters of conquest. Rivers are meeting places. Rivers turn us inward while oceans set us adrift. My Wiradjuri sister, the author Anita Heiss, has written beautifully of our rivers and how they connect us. Of the stories that travel on the waters. In her novel *Bila Yarrudhanggalangdhuray*, she tells of the White cockatoos flocking by the river's edge; our river the Murrumbidgee. She tells of invasion and the curse of Whiteness. She writes in our language that she learned from our old people and she tells of survival and family and love. Above all she tells of love.

Today by the Murrumbidgee, with love all around me, it is just like the first morning. Darkness turning to light. The wonder of it all. Precious, precious life that may not exist anywhere else in the universe. I don't know. Science, I am sure, will one day explain it all. How just the right chemical and physical mix made all of this possible. Science has unlocked so many of the secrets of existence. Physicists have smashed together heavy ions to recreate the plasma of quarks and gluons brought into existence right at the moment of the Big Bang. We can see almost to the very beginning. We have discovered the Higgs boson: God's particle.

My people tell us about Baiame, who came from the skies with his wife Birrahgnooloo and had a son, Darramulum. Baiame, our creation ancestor, gave rules to the people. In Genesis we are told how God created everything under heaven. The Bible tells me we – humans in God's image – have dominion over it all. And so we have subdued the Earth. Like Prometheus, we have stolen fire itself. We have become death, the destroyer of worlds. So what is our dominion without love? That is the curse of humankind.

These are the stories I was raised on. Stories of my people and the stories I heard in church. Stories peoples the world over have told themselves to try to grasp the awesome mystery of it all. Mythology, faith, the spirit world, science and reason – I wrestle with it all. It all lives in me. There is folly in thinking I can ever understand it fully. Science and reason cannot fill the God-shaped hole in me. What I feel here, by this river, cannot be captured in an equation. Poetry can get me close, but there are no words equal to the dancing butterfly. So here, now, I just want to let it be and fall into the reverie.

Some people like to think that we can return to some place and time that puts things to rights. It is a common trope in literature. The person who returns home. In these stories we wander, lost, until we find our way back. There we can be complete. It sounds good, doesn't it? I understand the need. The ache to become whole again. I understand it especially for those of my people who feel the tear in time.

I don't want to put that burden on my country. I don't need to. It is enough for me that I am here. Lost, confused, sad and joyful, all at once. This place does not want anything more from me. It holds all that I am. All the broken pieces. Especially the broken pieces.

Home. I have come and I have gone. Exile is the state of the restless, wandering soul. I have gone in search of answers since the time I began to ask *why*. Why us? Why did fate land such heavy blows? Why do we do the things we do to one another? Why am I Black? Why are others White? Why history? Why time? Why faith? Why hope? Why, why, why? All these questions have taken me so far from the place I love. From the people I love. These questions plague me. They torment me. These are the questions of modernity. This rapacious modernity. This irrepressible idea of freedom, so enticing, yet it can leave us shipwrecked and untethered. Cast adrift. These aren't questions I would ever put to my parents. I would never need to. They slipped this curse. They know who they are.

There are no questions I can ask that don't feel so utterly small next to them and the beauty around me.

When I am home, I don't need to say much at all. It is enough that I am here. It is enough to know that my family is here. It is enough to know that time is all around me. It is enough to know that I can feel all my ancestors here. That I can reach through the universe and touch them. No heavy-ion collision can explain that. This is my home. Yet I cannot – I do not – stay. I come and I go. Each time it gets harder.

Today I feel like I never want to leave. I have always thought that when I die, this is where I will be. Here. To rest with my ancestors and leave no more. Now I know that I cannot wait until death – this is where I must be if I am to live. Only here can I feel truly alive. People talk about sovereignty, well this is what it means to me. To be here by this river with my ancestors all around me, where the animals know me and I can hear in the wind the language of my people. No flag, no anthem, no constitution can give this to me. No referendum can grant this. No one can take it from me. I know that forever there is a place on this Earth for me. This is my inheritance, and all I need to leave to my children. This is what is passed from my father to me.

❊

The White Queen is dead.

Wiray ngiyang. Wiray mayinyi.

No language. No people.

This week, I heard my people speak. I heard my language. This week, I know we are still here. Here on Wiradjuri Ngurambang. I was struck again by the sheer miracle of it. The heroism of a people to keep holding on. Our survival was no given thing. At times my people have faced being wiped off the face of the Earth. Not by accident. Not by nature. By a systematic attempt to erase us. To wash us away on the tides of history.

Wars were fought on my country. Martial law was declared on my people. Exterminating wars, they were called.

Australians are only now beginning to learn about it. To accept that there was no peaceful settlement here. We did not melt into the shadows. We were not passive. We did resist. And the spirits of those people are here still. Let anyone sit quietly with themselves here and deny that.

There was a time our language was silenced. But our old people held strong. They kept it alive. This week, the latest class of the postgraduate Wiradjuri language and culture program graduated from Charles Sturt University. Among them were family. My sister. My daughter. Cousins and aunties. There, at the centre of it all, was my father, Stan Grant senior or as we call him, Yemarran Budhung – the Black Horse. I have his name – Stan – but I have never filled it out like he has.

I watch them wheel him into the graduation hall. Old now and frail. Fading. But there he is, strong in spite of it all. And as unsteady as he is, his people are there for him to lean on. A strong, young, proud Wiradjuri man with a flowing beard and long hair pushes Dad's wheelchair. He sits next to him on stage. He won't let him falter. There are other Wiradjuri people there with him too. My Uncle Pat speaks to the room. Yirradhu marang. Good morning. He welcomes everyone to Wiradjuri country and our words fill the hall.

It was almost gone, our language. Now it lives again. It is taught in schools. Dad made a point of going into our jails, where far too many of our people languish, and teaching people how to speak back to a world that had never heard them. Had never listened to them.

One by one the graduates receive their certificates, and each one embraces Dad. There are tears in their eyes. And there are tears in mine. And, in these moments, fear too. What will we do without him? What will we do without all of our elders, our culture and knowledge keepers? I can't think of myself as an elder. Not yet. Not like my father. I am not ready. I don't know if I ever could be.

❅

Bumaldhaany Babiin.

Listen to those words.

Each night, I would drive past the Royal Prince Alfred Hospital in Sydney, wind down my window and yell those same words.

Bumaldhaany Babiin.

My father was in the neurology ward; he had lost his speech and his movement. He had taken a heavy fall and suffered a severe brain trauma. The bleeding had formed a clot. He was eighty years old and there was no guarantee he would come back from this.

Bumaldhaany Babiin.

The Bumaldhaany are our warriors. My father is my Babiin. Somewhere in that hospital, I knew, he could hear me. Covid-19 restrictions meant that I could not see him in the intensive-care unit. Only my mother was allowed in. But my Babiin – my father – could hear me. I was sure of that. Our language would find him, and he would fight, because that's what Wiradjuri warriors do: we fight.

He had been sick before. He had already undergone brain surgery for a benign cyst. He had been in deep pain. Every part of his body ached and he suffered blinding headaches. In his quiet moments he had told my uncle he didn't know if he could go on. Or if he even wanted to.

Then the magpie came. Garru. He saw it in a dream. There was a flock of them on the front lawn of his house and they were talking. The garru were Dad's father and his grandfather. They spoke to him in our language, and they told him it wasn't his time. There was more he had to do.

This is what he lives for. Moments like this. A dream that our people would speak and stay alive. Drive across this part of the country now and there are signs reminding us that this is Wiradjuri country. In that graduation hall, White people spoke our language too. As it should be. As my father wants it to be. When my father talks about his people, he is not just talking about Wiradjuri people but anyone on Wiradjuri land. Our language, our strength, our culture, our kinship comes from place. A deep, deep connection to place.

I have searched the world over for an answer to that question I can't shake: what do we do after catastrophe? Here is my answer. We give back love. We find words to speak love. Vengeance, resentment – what does that do? Evil begets evil. The victim today is the perpetrator tomorrow. And on it goes. That's where we are different. If there is one thing I would say to those people who ask me what it is to be Aboriginal, I would tell them it is love. When hope seems lost, and it often does, there is love. It is a love that is not sentimental. Not just love for enemies but love because love lives inside us. This rescues me from the word games of Whiteness; from nihilism. Nihilism comes easy on a full stomach. But in the burning hunger of our despair, that's when we find the true meaning of our love.

The Australian anthem is played in the graduation hall. This song doesn't speak to me. I stand for it. I show respect to others. But I don't sing it. How could I? What is there for us to rejoice? We changed the words from 'young and free' to 'one and free' as if that would make it all right. But are we free? Can we say we are one? No. Not yet. Maybe we should not pursue it at all. I know where that leads. To create one out of many so easily falls into tyranny.

Anthems are more often performed than felt. But today there is something different. It is like I am hearing this anthem anew. The people I hear do not sing it with triumph in their voices but with humility, because in that room there is something more enduring than an anthem or a flag. Our words have joined with these words, and in that space we are joined – all of us, people who have come from so many lands. I watch Uncle Pat sing and I feel churlish for not joining in. My silent protest, which I tell myself is so righteous, now feels petulant.

It was the day after the graduation ceremony that I came to sit by the river near my parents' house. There I took it all in. I breathed it in. In the quiet, with my heart still, I came alive. I said to a friend of mine: the world makes sense for me here. It does. In a profound way. And if sometimes it doesn't, then that's okay too. It doesn't always have to make sense. It is enough that I can breathe here, given I struggle for breath when I am away. Coming home fills me up.

Balladhu Wiradjuri Gibir. I am a Wiradjuri man.

Dyirrimadalinya Badhu Wiradjuri. Proudly Wiradjuri.

This is what it means to have a voice. A voice that comes from my people. That comes from my father, and all of our fathers and mothers before them. From those people in that graduation hall. The Voice. It has become such a political thing. I hear words of politics and I want to dive into the river and wash myself clean. Politics shrinks us. No one I hear today speaks of politics. No one.

I am in a place bigger than politics. This is a place of love.

Love of language. Love of people. Love of country.

Wiray ngiyang. Wiray mayinyi. Without language we are not a people.

Until we can speak to each other in this land, this place Australia, can we ever call ourselves a people?

❖

The White Queen is dead.

How silly to think this land was empty. *Terra nullius*. How do you build a nation on that? What a truly miserable idea. Most Australians would not be aware that 'the skeleton of Australian law' says that this place was an uncultivated desert. That's how Britain claimed it. They could not hear and they could not see. And they certainly could not see us. Still they cannot. And it is sad. Because when they see us, I really believe they may see themselves.

How silly to think that becoming a republic would give us meaning. What would it be to replace the monarchy with an Australian head of state? Would we not be the same nation?

Would we not still be a nation built on emptiness? An Australian republic would be the completion of the vision of Stan Parker, Patrick White's first Australian, who cleared the land with an axe. From that first foreign sound in the forest, we built all that we can see. A republic would just make it ours. Or, more particularly, yours. More assuredly yours. Would a republic matter to me? Would the river flow any differently? Would the birds sing more sweetly? I don't need Australia to be a republic to belong here. Let them get rid of the Crown. It matters nothing to me. But without justice for First Nations, while ever we suffer, then *republic* is just another word, like *discovery* or *invasion* or *settlement* or *colony*. Just another for word for *Australia*.

Here, where I sit by a river and absorb the timeless beauty of place, these things of politics wither. They hold nothing for me here. Oh, the futile impermanence of it all. That's what catastrophe teaches us: that these things we think of as everlasting can be obliterated. The truths of tens of thousands of years splintered two centuries ago for my people. Two centuries ago, there was no such place as Australia. In two centuries from now, who is to say what will remain? What will the people of the future call this place? Look at a map of Europe from the dawn of the twentieth century and lay over it a map of today. Entire nations, things that people lived and fought and died for, have gone.

When Australians have been asked if they want to become a republic, they have said no. They cannot even agree on what a republic might be. For what it's worth, if we were asked again, I would vote yes. I would like to think we can be our own people. Change the flag, too. Find an anthem that we can all sing. Yes. Do all of those things. Or not. Do nothing. Stay as we are. It won't change who I am.

Isn't there a bigger question here? How do we find peace in a place where we still cannot truly speak to each other? Some say we are a nation of parts: Indigenous heritage, British foundation, filled out by the cultural richness and renewal of migration. In the sum of those parts, it is said, we can find something new. It sounds good. People – especially White people – like to hear this. But it sounds convenient, like a compromise. It sounds like politics to me. It is a beautiful idea of Australia but we haven't earned it. Anyway it is the wrong way around. We are part of a place. We are part of the waters and rocks and trees and earth and birds and animals and languages that grew out of this place. What good a republic? What good a thing called Australia? That's who we are. We have to bring meaning to that. Before a republic, we have to know what it means to be here. We have to know first where we are.

How silly to think that God would anoint a White King. To think that holy oil would bless this man. Whatever God is, it is not this. I know God. I see God now, right in front of me. We have our own word for God: Baiame. It is the creator. The spirit that lives in the skies. I know the God of the little white mission church that is always a part of me. I know that God is not a God of triumph. And I know it is not a God of Whiteness.

People say that Christianity is the foundation of the West. Yes, it is the basis of law. Of culture. But Christianity is not the possession of the West. Faith is not law. It is not nation. And it is certainly not some place we can draw on a map. Where is Jesus in what we call the West? It has always seemed obscene to me to take someone who stood against tyranny and empire – someone who spoke only of love – and put him in the service of conquest. But that's the White Jesus. This is not Christianity, it is Christendom. Christendom is the Rosetta Stone of the West, an encrypted message of Western superiority. The triumphalist West still believes this. This is the empire of a White Christ. This is God at the head of armies. This is the divine right of kings and queens. This is a papal decree that any land not governed by a Christian monarch is free for the taking.

I am a Christian and I find no home in White Christendom. The faith I was raised in – that beautiful Wiradjuri harmony carried on the voices of a people forsaken – found a place with God in spite of everything Christendom had brought. Ours is the crucified Christ; crucified as a political act. Our theology is political, but it is not White politics. Not the politics that leaves me depleted. It is a theology of liberation. And it is Black. My uncle who preached in Black churches across New South Wales always said he was a Wiradjuri Christian. He said he did not follow a failed European Christianity. How could he?

It is unfashionable to talk about Christ and God and faith. In the West there is a turn against religion. I understand that impulse. The Church has debased so much of what it should believe in. It has wrought untold harm on innocence. It is infected with politics. Charlatans and conmen turn God into a banker. I want nothing of that.

I pity those who use faith to mask their bigotry. Those who scour scripture looking for ways to judge others. I wonder how they arrive at such certainty. They are certainly not reading the perplexing, confusing, confounding, enraging, enlightening and enlarging Bible that I read. I wonder why they stop asking questions. My faith is not about questioning who people love, rejecting others or telling them what is the pathway to God because I am still searching for that myself. Some seek to defend their faith on a mound of exclusion, I will defend my faith on the mountain of grace, love, forgiveness, humility and kindness that I get on bended knee to ask for every day.

Some people may reach for the spiritual but not religion. But religion matters to me. Spirituality is too opaque. It sounds like something we can choose. It sounds like an experiment. Like a lifestyle. There is not enough suffering in it for me. Religion is an affirmation of the spiritual. It asks something of me. I need to commit. I need to accept doctrine and yet push against dogma. I have to live with doubt and things that are incomprehensible, yet try to comprehend them anyway. I find solace in faith. I find it in places of worship. I find it in mosques and temples and homes brimming with love. I find it by a river and under a tree. I find it in churches. Yes, especially in church. I find it in a Nick Cave song.

I have my faith and I don't hold that over others. I respect their paths to transcendence wherever they find them. There are people of no faith, too, who are good and loving. There is in humanity a struggle between our best and our worst, and I have seen our worst triumph far too often, so whatever leads us to our best – music, poetry, nature, the touch of those we love, even just the everyday – I find praise in that. But I have not found answers in the secular world to the questions I ask. That is for God. For me, it is found in God.

I could not find the love to stare into the face of history without hate if I did not have God. If I did not carry with me always and forever the voices of that little white wooden mission church. Oh, the forsaken. That little church of the crucified Christ. That rupture in the universe when God became us. Took the pain and suffering and offered us eternity.

I know it is hard for some people to read these things. Especially people of no faith. But we live, all of us – the faithful and the faithless – in the shadow of the cross. Even those of other faiths live in a world informed by that moment. Even those gospelling, proselytising atheists. Their disbelief or even disregard for faith is their own faith. Their atheism is theistic. It dismisses the supernatural God in the heavens, God above humans, as superstition. They scoff at miracles yet miss the miracles all around us; the miracles of our world; the miracle that we are. They may believe that the world – love even – can be captured in a mathematical equation. But to me love is divine. It is the love of the cross.

❈

The White Queen is dead.

I go for a run. I love that turn from day to dusk, and I follow the path from my parents' home back along the river and up into the town. Then I hear a sound. Voices. People singing. And I recognise the melody. I stop and look across at a stone church. There, in a circle, are a handful of people. They strum guitars and together their voices seem to blend into one. 'O Come, All Ye Faithful' – I love that hymn. There, in that moment, it is even more beautiful. They are not in church but outside it. They are under a tree. And they are singing for the sheer joy of it all. For the love of it all. It takes me back to the little White church on the mission. Back to when I was a boy.

But these people are not Black people. They are not Wiradjuri. They are White. Does that matter? Yes, it does. There is a history between us. There is still a divide that can feel like a chasm. There are so many ways I would not understand them, nor they me. We come to God in our own way. We read the same scriptures but they speak to us differently. I have been in White churches and I have always felt slightly out of place. Not unwelcome, not at all, but as if I am a day out.

These are the people of Easter Sunday, the triumphant resurrection and my people are of the dark Saturday; the day after the crucifixion. On that day God is dead to the world. This is the darkness of our suffering and in that darkness God is with us as he was with Jesus in the moment of abandonment. And in the risen Christ, is the God of love, not a God above us or beyond us, not a God of which we are unworthy, but a God within us. As Jurgen Moltmann has written: 'God suffers, God allows himself to be crucified and is crucified, and in this consummates his unconditional love that is so full of hope.'

Love leads us home and love leads us to each other. And love leads me here to these voices. Then, there, in that place, these people are singing on Wiradjuri land under a tree outside a church. And I hear them.

I needed to hear them. My faith tells me God put me here right at that moment because I needed to hear them. To others it may just be coincidence. Perhaps at another time I may have just passed by. But this is the journey I have been on. Since the death of the White Queen I have wrestled with anger, resentment, betrayal, sadness and return; return home and to find a place of love and peace. My faith which has always been there has been deepened and strengthened by the ordeal.

In truth I have been on this journey all my life. All those little towns. Those questions without answers. The peace I find by a river or listening to my people speak our language or hearing a hymn, is a peace that eludes our country still. There is too much suffering, too much pain; too little justice. But there is always love. Love that keeps my people alive.

Ngiyang. Mayinyi. Language. People.

16

LET IT GO

The White Queen is dead.

I am in a room with so many other people, all of us here to listen to a man sing his pain. The man in a three-piece black suit like an undertaker or a preacher. His arms outstretched and his body writhing and turning. He turns this place into a holy place. We are a room of strangers, at least in that we don't know each other. But we are not strangers to the human in us. All of us. Each feels what the others feel. That connects us. We are here for connection. Or we wouldn't be here at all. We need to know there is something else in our world, something that might save us.

I am sitting alongside my son. I can feel the touch of him as he brushes my arm – and the touch of all those who have come before us, all of our ancestors reaching back to the beginning of human time, who have put us here in this moment together. They are all here with us too. In him I go on. And he will go on.

I am here with him because we share the love of music. But there's another reason. I am here with him because I want to hold these moments close. Because he is so precious to me. And the man on the stage is singing about the son he has lost. The son taken too soon from the Earth. And he is looking for a way to go on. After the world stops, he tries to find a way to smile again. Poetry after catastrophe. If we can't write it, what is there for us? This man, he is here because he knows that death is not the final word. Love is. Love is the final word.

Nick Cave has been the voice I have heard so often as I have written. He inhabits the world of ghosts too. Just like me. He has followed the questions of faith wherever they lead. Just like me. And they have led to some dark places. His music has always been a companion, but there's more now – it tingles in me now. There is a wisdom, a worn-out wisdom. There is silence in between the notes, and that is what I listen for. That is where the hope is. In the space before we have filled it. Like the Sistine Chapel and the space between the outreached hands of Adam and God. That's where we live, all of us. Just a touch away, and all of us existing in the reaching.

Love. The questions that have sent me around the world have returned me to this truth: love. When I think about it now, it was always pointing in this direction. My eyes have turned so often and so easily to horror. If you pursue the worst, the worst is what you will find. And it is not hard to find. Victor Hugo wrote that for thousands of years war has pleased the quarrelling peoples of the Earth, and God has wasted his time making the stars and the flowers. I have let wars turn my eyes away from the stars and the flowers. And then I would see love. A spark of love in the worst places.

Like the time I sat in a tent in the middle of a field in Pakistan with a family who had lost everything. Their elder son was dead. Their younger son was badly injured. The father had carried his wounded boy down the side of a mountain. Here they were. A mother cooking over an open fire. Living inside a makeshift tent. All they had in the world. But so much love. We could not speak to each other – not in language, at least. But we spoke in love.

When the mother finished cooking, she dished up a plate and offered it first to me. A stranger. She offered love first to a stranger. This woman who had just lost her son. Oh, love. Oh my god, love.

The White Queen is dead.

I have had to break to find a way back to love. Elizabeth, this woman who shared a Queen's name. My mother, Elizabeth, a girl with no socks who saw the Queen. She led me back to love. Her words. Her stories. Her little stories about a family of White and Black, just holding on. Her parents, Keith and Ivy, their love that shattered and yet stayed. Her brother Kevin, who wrote to tell me our story. When a nation buried its truth in lies, he bothered to write. Just to keep love alive.

There are many years in my father, and his people are with him. That man who is wheeled into a hall where people can speak our language because of him. And because he would not let it be silenced. Because he loved his grandfather, he would not let it go. And this land held the language within it, and it couldn't die while we walked on this land. I drove him home from the graduation ceremony and I watched him drift in and out of sleep. He sleeps a lot now, and easily. And in his sleep he reached out, his hands would raise and reach, just like he could touch forever.

Love. Love on long, dark nights on the road. Love in a dozen little towns where we took refuge. Love in the kindness of those who kept us alive. Love in the wooden church and the hymns of suffering and redemption and forgiveness. There is love in my life with a woman, my wife, who we might call White. There are times we don't understand each other; there is so much lost in translation. But we try. We always try. Because we love.

There is love beside a river.

There is enough love to tell me that God does not waste time among the stars and the flowers. The people who raised me believed there was enough love to build a nation on. Maybe.

❋

The White Queen is dead.

I watched the procession that took the Queen to her rest. There was love there too, I'm sure. She lived. She breathed. She suffered, like us all. She felt hope. There was love in the faces of her family. Love not for a monarch but for a mother.

We imagine history as a grand sweep. But it isn't. It is just the collection of small lives.

The love of her family was more real than the myths of the monarchy. There is no love in the myths of empire. The myths of Whiteness have no room for love. How can they? How can we suppose that a tiny fraction of the planet can conquer us all? How can we put God in the service of racism?

The White Queen's life wrapped around mine, around all of our lives. I have no hatred, no bitterness towards her. But I do have sadness. It is a sadness for what that crown did to my people; to my family. It is a sadness for a world that I have seen up close far too often in all of its horror. That world scarred by empire. It is a sadness that Australia feels less like a nation and more like an imposition, because we fail; we fail ourselves every day.

I watched the Queen lowered into the vault in the grand church. She was entombed in royalty. And then it was sealed shut. And that was it. Just like us all, she lived and she is gone. Nothing more. Nothing but what we might imagine.

Let it go. Let the spell be broken.

The White Queen is dead.

LIST OF REFERENCES

Adorno, Theodore. *Prisms*, The MIT Press, 1983.

Allen, Theodore W. *The Invention of the White Race, Volume 1*, Verso, 2012.

Australian Human Rights Commission. *Bringing them Home Report*, 1997.

Baldwin, James. *Notes of a Native Son*, Penguin Classics, [1955] 2018.

Cave, Nick & O'Hagan, Sean. *Faith, Hope and Carnage*, Text Publishing, 2022.

Ch'en, Jerome. *China and the West: Society and Culture, 1815–1937*, Hutchinson & Co., 1979.

Coates, Te-Nehisi. *Between the World and Me*, One World, 2015.

Deleuze, G. *Difference and Repetition*, trans. Paul Patton, Columbia University Press, 1968.

Derrida, Jacques. *Specters of Marx: The State of the Debt*, Routledge, 1994.

Douglass, Frederick. *July Fourth Oration* delivered in Rochester, New York, 5 July 1852.

Du Bois, W.E.B. *The Souls of Black*, A.C. McClurg & Co., 1903.

Eliot, T.S. 'The Wasteland', 1922.

Elizabeth II, 'A speech by the Queen on her 21st birthday', 21 April 1947.

Elkins, Caroline. *Legacies of Violence: A History of the British Empire*, Knopf, 2022.

Ellison, Ralph, *Invisible Man*, 1952.

Fanon, Frantz. 'The Fact of Blackness', in Les Back & John Solomos, *Theories of Race and Racism: A Reader*, Routledge, 2009.

Fields, Barbara J. & Fields, Karen E. *Racecraft: The Soul of Inequality in American Life*, Verso, 2014.

Gilroy, P. *The Black Atlantic: Modernity and Double Consciousness*, Harvard University Press, 1993.

Glissant, Édouard. *Poetics of Relation*, The University of Michigan Press, 1990.

Hegel, George Wilhelm Friedrich. *The Phenomenology of Spirit*, 1807.

Hirsch, Afua. *Brit(ish): On Race, Identity and Belonging*, Jonathan Cape, 2018.

Hooks, Bell. *All About Love: New Visions*, William Morrow, 1999.

Horn, Jonathan. '"Black and proud": remembering the day Nicky Winmar changed footy forever', *The Guardian*, 16 April 2018.

Kant, Immanuel. 'What is Enlightenment?', 1784.

King, Dr Martin Luther. 'Why America May Go to Hell', 7 April 1968.

Lear, Jonathan. *Radical Hope*, Harvard University Press, 2006.

Malcolm X. *Message to the Grassroots*, speech given at a rally in Detroit, Michigan, 1963.

Markle, Meghan. 'I'm More Than An "Other"', *Elle*, 22 December 2016.

Milosz, Czeslaw. *Nobel Lecture*, 8 December 1980.

Mishra, Pankaj. *From the Ruins of Empire*, Picador, 2013.

Moltmann, Jurgen. *The Crucified God: The Cross of Christ as the Foundation and Criticism of Christian Theology*, trans. R A. Wilson & John Bowden, Fortress Press, 1973, 1993.

Nietzsche, Friedrich. *On the Genealogy of Morals*, 1887.

Pawel, Ernst. *The Nightmare of Reason: A Life of Franz Kafka*, Farrar, Straus & Giroux, 1984.

Pearson, Noel. 'Who we were, who we are, and who we can be', *Boyer Lectures*, Australian Broadcasting Corporation, 4 November 2022.

Rawls, John. *A Theory of Justice: Revised Edition*, Belknap Press, 1999.

Reece, R.H.W. 'Inventing Aboriginies', in V. Chapman & P. Read, *Terrible Hard Biscuits*, Routledge, 1996.

Reich, David. *Who We Are and How We Got Here: Ancient DNA and the New Science of the Human Past*, Oxford University Press, 2019.

Ridley, John. 'A True Champion vs. The "Great White Hope"', NPR, 2 July 2010.

Said, Edward. *Out of Place: A Memoir*, Vintage, 2000.

Sanders, Katie. 'Did Vladimir Putin call the breakup of the USSR "the greatest political tragedy of the 20th century"', politifact. com, 6 March 2014.

Schiller, Friedrich von. 'Resignation', 1786.

Scott, Lynn O. *James Baldwin's Later Fiction: Witness to the Journey*, Michigan State University Press, 2002.

Shakespeare, William. *Hamlet*, ed. G.R. Hibbard, Oxford University Press, 2008.

Sondheim, Stephen. 'America', *West Side Story*, 1957.

Stovall, T.E. *White Freedom: The Racial History of an Idea*, Princeton University Press, 2021.

Trump, Donald. '2017 Donald Trump inauguration speech transcript', politico, 20 January 2017.

United Nations, *Convention on the Prevention and the Punishment of the Crime of Genocide*, General Assembly Resolution 260 A (III), ratified 9 December 1948, entered into force 12 January 1951.

Ward, Geoffrey. *Unforgivable Blackness: The Rise and Fall of Jack Johnson*, Jonathan Cape, 2004.

Weil, Simone. *Gravity and Grace*, 1946.

Weil, Simone. *Waiting for God*, 1950.

West, Cornel. 'Hope and Despair: Past and Present', in Tommie Shelby & Brandon M. Terry, *To Shape a New World*, Harvard University Press, 2018.

Wilson, Monica & Thompson, Leonard. *The Oxford History of South Africa*, Clarendon Press, 1971.

Wolf, Miroslav. *Exclusion and Embrace: A Theological Exploration of Identity, Otherness, and Reconciliation*, Abingdon Press, 1996.

Yeats, W.B. 'The Second Coming', *The Collected Poems of W.B. Yeats*, [1920] 1989.

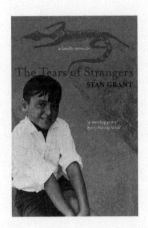

THE TEARS OF STRANGERS

Stan Grant was born in 1963 into the Wiradjuri people, warriors who occupied the vast territory of central and south-western New South Wales. For 100 years the Wiradjuri waged a war against European invasion and settlement. When Stan was born the war had been lost, the remnants of the Wiradjuri were scattered onto mission camps and the fringes of rural towns, and ravaged by alcoholism, poverty, abuse and neglect. Against this backdrop the Grant family waged its own struggle to survive.

From first contact with White settlers to today, *The Tears of Strangers* is an unforgettable Aboriginal memoir of survival, healing and hope. It is the story of the Wiradjuri people, the Grant family and Stan's own journey to come to terms with his Aboriginality and identity.

'a serious, considered and, above all, honest portrait of both his own life and Australians' attitudes to race.'
– *The Age*

TALKING TO MY COUNTRY

Talking to My Country is Stan Grant's very personal meditation on race, identity and history. It is that rare and special book that talks to every Australian about their country – what it is, and what it could be. It is not just about race, or about Indigenous people but all of us, our shared identity. Direct, honest and forthright, Stan is talking to us all. He might not have all the answers but he wants us to keep on asking the question: how can we be better?

'an urgent and flowing narrative in a book that should be on the required reading list in every school' – *The Australian*

'Grant will be an important voice in shaping this nation' – *The Saturday Paper*

AUSTRALIA DAY

As uncomfortable as it is, we need to reckon with our history. On January 26, no Australian can really look away. There are the hard questions we ask of ourselves on Australia Day.

Since publishing his critically acclaimed, Walkley Award-winning, bestselling memoir *Talking to My Country* in early 2016, Stan Grant has been crossing the country, talking to huge crowds everywhere about how racism is at the heart of our history and the Australian dream. But Stan knows this is not where the story ends.

In this book, *Australia Day*, his long-awaited follow up to *Talking to My Country*, Stan talks about our country, about who we are as a nation, about the indigenous struggle for belonging and identity in Australia, and what it means to be Australian. A sad, wise, beautiful, reflective and troubled book, *Australia Day* asks the questions that have to be asked, that no else seems to be asking. Who are we? What is our country? How do we move forward from here?

'a soulful meditation on who we are by an Australian whose emotional and intellectual range is as vast as the ochreous land itself' – *The Australian*

WITH THE FALLING OF THE DUSK

In only a few short decades, we have come a long way from Francis Fukuyama's declaration of the 'end of history' and the triumph of liberal democracy in 1989. Now, with the inexorable rise of China, the ascendancy of authoritarianism and the retreat of democracy, the world stands at a moment of crisis. This is a time of momentous upheaval and enormous geopolitical shifts, compounded by the global pandemic, economic collapse and growing inequality, Islamist and far right terror, and a resurgent White supremacy. The world is in lockdown and the showdown with China is accelerating - and while the West has been at the forefront of history for 200 years, it must now adapt to a world it no longer dominates. At this moment, we stand on a precipice - what will become of us?

Stan Grant is one of our foremost observers and chroniclers of the world in crisis. Weaving his personal experiences of reporting from the front lines of the world's flashpoints, together with his deep understanding of politics, history and philosophy, he explores what is driving the world to crisis and how it might be averted. He fears the worst, but begins to chart the way forward. There is bitterness, anger and history here, but there is also the capacity for negotiation, forgiveness and hope. A powerful and incisive analysis of the state of our world, and our place within it.